FOOD ADULTERATION AND FOOD FRAUD

FOOD CONTROVERSIES

SERIES EDITOR: ANDREW F. SMITH

Everybody eats. Yet few understand the importance of food
in our lives and the decisions we make each time we eat.
The Food Controversies series probes problems created by
the industrial food system and examines proposed alternatives.

Already published:

Fast Food: The Good, the Bad and the Hungry Andrew F. Smith
Food Adulteration and Food Fraud Jonathan Rees
What's So Controversial about Genetically Modified Food? John T. Lang
What's the Matter with Meat? Katy Keiffer

FOOD ADULTERATION AND FOOD FRAUD

JONATHAN REES

REAKTION BOOKS

Published by Reaktion Books Ltd
Unit 32, Waterside
44–48 Wharf Road
London N1 7UX, UK

www.reaktionbooks.co.uk

First published 2020
Copyright © Jonathan Rees 2020

Printed and bound in India by Replika Press Pvt. Ltd

A catalogue record for this book is available from the British Library
ISBN 978 1 78914 194 8

CONTENTS

INTRODUCTION:
A MATTER OF TRUST *7*

1 PARTIAL SUBSTITUTIONS *25*

2 TAINTED FOODS *42*

3 COUNTERFEIT FOODS AND COMPLETE
SUBSTITUTIONS *60*

4 THE IMPORTANCE OF PLACE *77*

5 TESTING *94*

6 POLICY, STRATEGY AND LEGISLATION *109*

CONCLUSION: ADULTERATION AND CULTURE *126*

REFERENCES *145*
NOTE ON SOURCES AND SELECT BIBLIOGRAPHY *165*
INDEX *171*

INTRODUCTION: A MATTER OF TRUST

Eating food prepared, manufactured or cooked by some-one else has always been an act of trust. In the Middle Ages and Renaissance, royal families required food tasters because they were afraid of poisoning. These days the effects of whatever poisons might be in our foods tend to take effect much more slowly. Over time, what we eat (and what we don't) has lasting effects upon our lives and our health. Thus eating is an intimate act. Unless we happen to be farmers or gardeners, we take something produced, handled and often cooked by someone else and put it into our mouths – we take it into our bodies. That is perhaps the easiest explanation for why some people choose what they eat so carefully, while others trust food producers unfailingly (if not consciously).

Today, even if people aren't being poisoned by their food, there is nevertheless a good chance they are being cheated. People once depended upon visual clues to know if the food they bought was spoiled or altered somehow. If a baker added sawdust to his flour in order to stretch it further, it was impossible to tell until you brought the bread home and cracked it open. Even today, consumers are not equipped with chemical testing kits when they go to the supermarket. They have to depend upon the farmers, producers and merchants who sell them food to be trustworthy; otherwise customers would cease to do business with them, and commerce would grind to a halt.

As food-provisioning systems have grown larger and more complicated, producers and consumers have become more physically separated. Indeed, there are often whole oceans between the producers and consumers of particular foods. This greater complexity in provisioning systems also means that consumers have become less likely to understand anything about what goes into the products they eat. This in turn makes it easier for food producers to slip in ingredients that don't belong or to substitute entirely different foods in order to make more money. For consumers to decide which ingredients should be welcome in a particular food requires a decision about exactly what that food is. To answer that question requires an examination of what function that food performs and whether an entirely different set of ingredients can perform that function just as well. It might also require some consideration of where that food originates.

The traditional name for any kind of manipulation of food products is food adulteration. Dishonest sellers can adulterate food at any point along the supply chain so that they can pocket the price difference between the adulterant and the unadulterated food they leave out. When one dishonest seller undercuts the price of a good, other producers may feel the pressure to adulterate their products too so that they can cut prices to a similar level. In this manner, a few bad apples can undermine the quality of whole subsections of food industries. Because food supply chains are often global, food adulteration is an international problem. Examine food adulteration anywhere in the world and you are looking at a practice that might very well affect what you buy at your local supermarket, if not directly, then indirectly.

Estimates of the extent of food adulteration, and its close cousin food fraud, are obviously difficult to make because these deceptions are difficult to detect. Nonetheless, there is wide agreement that the problem is severe and growing worse all the time. 'Around the world, food fraud is an epidemic – in every single country where food is produced or grown, food fraud is occurring,' explained the president of a private firm that advises on food security issues in 2013. 'Just about every single ingredient that has even a moderate economic value is potentially vulnerable to fraud.'[1]

According to the Grocery Manufacturers Association, food fraud of all kinds costs food producers worldwide somewhere between $10 billion and $15 billion per year.[2] In Great Britain, it has been estimated that this practice costs UK firms £11 billion each year.[3] In the United States, as much as 10 per cent of the food on supermarket shelves might be adulterated.[4] In Bangladesh, the problem of food adulteration is so bad that it has been likened to genocide.[5] One of the problems with assessing the extent of food fraud is that there is no really reliable data on the extent of the problem. Some of the information generated about the problem is proprietary, or kept secret for fear of lawsuits. Even the definitions of 'food adulteration' and 'food fraud' vary from country to country.[6]

Among the foods that most often get adulterated or fraudulently marketed are fish, honey, olive oil, chilli powder and milk. While none of these foods are particularly expensive, they are all sufficiently so that it pays either to partially substitute in cheaper ingredients or to misrepresent something else entirely as the good in question. Other popular foods to adulterate, such as caviar, are expensive enough that money can be made by adulterating small amounts of the product. However, the fact that there is a market for adulterated rice or apple juice suggests the large scale at which adulteration can occur.[7]

Food Adulteration and Industrialization

Traditionally, food adulteration has been seen as the presence of any substance in a particular food that does not appear there naturally. A widely cited definition of food adulteration comes from the Food and Drug Administration (FDA) of the United States: 'the fraudulent, intentional substitution or addition of a substance in a product for the purpose of increasing the apparent value of the product or reducing the cost of its production'. While this is a good start, a broader definition of food adulteration would be more useful. Adulteration can also include just the removal of valuable substances that should appear in a food naturally. Moreover, by explicitly including some practices that are legal (albeit somewhat deceptive) in our working definition of adulteration, this activity can become a window into what food-manufacturing practices are acceptable across different cultures, and even into what food means to different people around the world.

Food adulteration can be traced all the way back to ancient times. The Romans complained about their wine being diluted. Greeks and Romans both complained that their wine had been artificially coloured. Adulteration was a problem in the earliest Chinese dynasties, too, around the second century BCE, while an old Sanskrit tablet from about 300 BCE threatens to fine anybody who adulterates grains, salts, oils, scents or medicines. The adulteration of flour with chalk also dates from the Greek and Roman era. Measures to control such practices are among the earliest recorded laws.[8] Nonetheless, these practices persisted.

However, it was only with industrialization and the mass production of foodstuffs that this problem became particularly bad. Industrialization meant that consumers became less familiar with the people who sold them food, which therefore made it far easier for producers to cheat them. When vegetables went into cans or whisky was put into brown bottles, consumers were no longer able to use traditional visual clues to see if the goods they were buying were actually pure. Today, packaging (often with deceptively delicious-looking pictures of the supposed contents) separates consumers from foods of all kinds. Even when they can see what they're buying, other inventions like artificial colourants make it easy to cover the signs of adulteration or decay that would have been easily detected in an earlier era.

Over the last 150 years or so, food manufacturing and food processing have become extraordinarily efficient, as well as technologically sophisticated. Since the late nineteenth century, as food manufacturing and processing has scaled up in different countries at different times, the separation between food producers and consumers has grown. Moreover, as people moved from the country to the city, they began to encounter new processed foods that they may never have seen before. This meant that it was particularly easy to fool consumers with adulterated foods, or even foods that were entirely fraudulent. Such deceptions included a vast variety of food products – everything from honey and beef to coffee and whisky.

Food additives, legal and illegal alike, have made the exact definition of food adulteration more fluid than it once was. To understand exactly why the line between adulterated and acceptable falls where it does, it is useful to examine both legal and illegal food adulteration. All food adulteration is an attack upon norms and a violation of the public trust.[9] In most instances, the success of the practice depends upon customers not knowing exactly what is in their food. While many consumers prefer ignorance about the exact nature of what they're eating, this is not always the case. In a similar way to vegetarians avoiding eating meat, health-conscious consumers will often avoid foods made with food additives that are perfectly legal to use because they believe they are unhealthy, even if their governments don't. This is a sign that public trust has already suffered severe harm.

Nobody supports food adulteration or food fraud (aside from the people making money from it). No ethical actors embrace these practices. However, there can be confusion at the margins about what these practices actually are. In fact, adulteration and even some kinds of deception can actually be welcomed by consumers, a situation that is of course predicated on the fact that they know these additions or subtractions from their food are actually happening. Any definition that does not take into account these other circumstances misses the many differences in how changes to food are perceived across cultures. It also misses the opportunity to see how ideas about what food should be have changed over time. The legal definition of adulteration is culturally determined, but laws seldom go as far as many cultures do. Whether adding something to food is legal or illegal depends upon how consumers react to this practice, which in turn depends upon whether they even know or understand that it is happening.

Food fraud is closely related to food adulteration, but is not quite the same thing. Think of it as a matter of degree: food adulteration is any substitution in or addition to a particular food and is only somewhat fraudulent, while food fraud that is not an adulteration involves a complete substitution and total deception. Food adulteration is a kind of food fraud, but there is far more adulteration than outright fraud because partial substitutions are much harder to detect than complete substitutions, as well as easier to justify if the perpetrator gets caught. It is very common in the reporting on this subject to fail to distinguish between adulterated and completely fraudulent foods. These two categories are obviously related, but they can be very different in practice. Adulteration usually involves simply adding something while a convincing complete substitute for any particular food can be much harder to find.[10]

Search scholarly and media databases for the term 'food adulteration' and its variants, and plenty of literature on food fraud and food adulteration will not appear in the results.[11] Nevertheless, thanks to a series of serious, well-reported incidents in recent years, food adulteration and food fraud have drawn important attention around the world. In less developed countries they are often literally a matter of life or death. However, the food in question does not necessarily have to be a threat to public health in order to be adulterated or fraudulent.[12]

The key to understanding the difference between legal and illegal practices involving food adulteration is the degree of deception involved. Place the cheaper ingredients on the label and price the resulting product lower, and it becomes more difficult to call the same practice food adulteration when the consumer is fully informed about what their food is made of. List all the ingredients on the label and, assuming the ingredient itself is legal, what you're doing is probably legal – if not necessarily ethical. How consumers react to food adulteration or food fraud depends upon their expectations of the risks they take when they eat something. Acceptable health risks in one country are unacceptable in others. These grey areas at the margins of acceptability are what reveal the cultural underpinnings of how people think about their food as well as the modern manufacturing practices that test the limits of which ingredients people are willing to consume.

Despite these differences, there are some kinds of food adulteration that are unacceptable everywhere. At the top of that list would be deliberate, fatal poisoning or anything close to bioterrorism exercised through the food supply. These crimes are incredibly rare compared to other forms of adulteration. Furthermore, such incidents are one-time events designed to inflict the greatest possible harm in the shortest possible time. Food adulteration and food fraud need to be an extended swindle in order to be profitable.[13] It is these kinds of deceptions that reveal the most about the societies where they occur. They also raise a lot of questions about the nature of food.

Types of Adulteration and Food Fraud

Every kind of food adulteration or food fraud threatens the trust that has to be maintained for the global food-provisioning system to function smoothly. Labels tell us what's in our food, but many incidents of adulteration remind us that those labels cannot always be trusted. The role of governments in this arrangement is to enforce the laws that food manufacturers have to follow, but this can be difficult when resources are at a premium and the food in question originates (as it so often does these days) somewhere outside its jurisdiction. Adulteration is intimately connected with public health since so many illegal additives are unhealthy or dangerous and so many legal ones are perceived to be. Examining food adulteration and food fraud also offers a unique opportunity for consumers to understand what exactly is in their food, and even what their food really is.

To explain why adulteration is important requires a taxonomy of the practice around the world. Classifying different kinds of adulteration will also help explain both why the practice occurs and its varying effects on economies and cultures at different stages of economic development. Many substances, like honey for example, are adulterated or sold fraudulently in a variety of different ways. Organizing by type of deception rather than food makes it possible to see the qualities of each kind of fraud that do not depend upon the food in question. Variations in these tactics suggest differences in culture too.

The most important dividing line between types of adulteration lies between economically motivated adulteration and fraud, and accidental or environmental contamination. 'Contamination and adulteration both may involve the presence of a substance that is not intended to be in a product,' explains the chemist Markus Lipp. 'The difference is that contamination is unintentional. It may result from natural causes . . . Contamination can also occur as a consequence of some sort of shortcoming or lapse in quality control.'[14] The important thing to remember is that from the point of view of the consumer the results of adulteration and accidental contamination are the same. Their health is threatened and the producer is at fault.

The earliest, pre-industrial adulterations were economic. They invariably involved substituting cheaper ingredients or fillers for a valuable pure food because it allowed producers or sellers to save money. Sell the adulterated food at the same price as the unadulterated food and a manufacturer's profits will increase sharply. A related swindle would be to short weight a customer when they bought your bread or wine, essentially adulterating your product with the cheapest additive of all, namely air. Pack a food in excess water or with too much ice and the effect can be the same. These kinds of dishonest practices date back to ancient times, and continue today wherever food is sold because capitalism incentivizes it. When profit is the seller's primary end and adulteration is hard to detect and potentially lucrative, it is bound to happen often.

A different kind of misrepresentation involves mislabelling or misbranding. Misrepresenting the country of origin for a particular food product might not involve adding anything to a product, but it is a serious breach of the trust because consumers often use country of origin as a sign of quality assurance. Because such mislabelled foods are often passed off for much more expensive products, this practice too can be very lucrative. Testing such products for type or their point of origin can be difficult and very expensive, meaning this kind of fraud can be very hard to detect. Only consumers with the most sophisticated palates might be able to tell the difference between such a product and the product it claims to be. Indeed, many victims of this fraud might prefer to think their high-end food purchases were legitimate products since their consumption is often as much a matter of status as it is of taste.

False or misleading claims about where a particular food is produced would also fit into this category of food fraud, even though they don't involve adulteration per se, since it means replacing one food with another that doesn't fit the label of the first food at all, even if the food is chemically similar in many ways. Trans-shipments, like moving Spanish olive oil to Italy and calling it Italian, are actually legal, but deceptive nonetheless. Misrepresenting the manufacturing process is another related form of deception. For example, claiming something is certified organic when it isn't will not necessarily hurt someone, but it is a kind of deception that resembles the food adulteration of old in the sense that it misrepresents a product for the sake of inflating profits. Other terms, like 'free range' or 'natural', are easy to use in a fraudulent manner because the production methods that can legally draw these labels are not always regulated and some of these terms are practically impossible to define.[15]

There are also problems with food documentation fraud in places where the production of particular foods is tightly controlled. The marketing and selling of legitimate food products in places where those foods aren't allowed is known as a diversion. When a legitimate food product is produced beyond the quantitative limits specified in production agreements it is known as an over-run.[16] These are not adulterations in the traditional sense of that word. They are food crimes designed to exploit the rules of today's global, highly regulated food-provisioning system. Like adulterations, however, these crimes are economically motivated and they depend upon the origins of a given food remaining mysterious.

The most disturbing kind of adulteration involves the addition of dangerous chemicals to food. In the early twentieth-century United States, people were suspicious of preservatives both because arresting decay was viewed as deceptive and because there were legitimate fears that some of them might not be healthy for people to consume over the course of a lifetime. The tendency of today's media to report that everything added to our food is a dangerous adulterant is just more evidence that reporters recognize that the easiest way to grab the public's attention is to write about either sex or death. Of course, some added ingredients really are dangerous, but it can be difficult for even the most informed consumers of news around the world to tell which ingredients those are.

Non-economically motivated forms of adulteration are usually best understood as contamination, a subcategory of adulteration. Their effects are the same as the most dangerous forms of adulteration, but their cause is either accidental or natural. Deliberate criminal behaviour is seldom involved. For example, illegally high amounts of pesticide residue have got into food products of all kinds in recent years. No producer in their right mind would let this happen intentionally, as such products become subject to costly recalls once their presence is detected. However, in this age of long supply chains, food producers and distributors have little control over exactly what happens to their products either before or after the food is under their direct control. These kinds of adulterations demonstrate the close link between this subject and food safety issues, a distinct but related food controversy that entails much more than just the ingredients of particular products.[17]

This book will not cover all of the different kinds of food adulteration to the same depth.[18] Some kinds of adulteration are more important than others because they happen more often or cause more damage. In fact, much of this book will examine practices that in many cultures are not considered to be adulterations at all. The location of the line between adulterated and acceptable is worth studying across cultures because it can reveal what different cultures expect their food to be. Equally, changes within cultures as to what is considered acceptable can, depending on one's perspective, mark either the degradation or modernization of that culture's diet.

It is also worth noting that plenty of foods can be subject to different kinds of adulteration at the same time. Olive oil, as we will see, variously gets watered down, poisoned, faked entirely and has its origins obscured. In theory at least, all of these things could happen simultaneously within a single shipment of oil. Because the following chapters are (mostly) organized around the type of adulteration rather than the food itself, olive oil and a few other foods will be mentioned in several places. The point here is not to scare anyone about the purity of a particular product, but to consider how the ways in which foods are adulterated inform us about what different societies find acceptable. Moreover, studying food adulteration methods can reveal how globalization has eroded the standards of purity in a lot of countries over recent years, without many consumers even recognizing that this was happening.

Between Adulterated and Acceptable

Because each culture has a basic understanding of what should or should not be in particular foods, adulteration will be defined at least slightly differently in different places. The key to understanding these variations is the cultural context in which potential adulterations appear. If a culture is permissive about how much food can be processed, or has little regulation over how its food gets made, it may allow changes that probably ought to be considered adulterations. If a culture is suspicious of food processing, it may overreact to changes in the ingredients that make up its food supply. People's under-standing of the relationship between food and well-being is also an important determinant of how consumers will react to changes in the way that food gets made. If people are worried about simply surviving, food adulteration will be low on their priority list. If they are privileged and health-conscious, they are likely to be deeply disturbed by changes in how food is manufactured; for them, any change in the traditional production process will seem like a dangerous adulteration.

When culture changes, so does the willingness of people to accept changes in how their food gets made. That is how foods that were once considered adulterated can end up becoming acceptable, and how things that are acceptable in one culture can become adulterations in another. Adulterations violate the rules, but the rules can be reset. Adulterated foods can become acceptable. Acceptable foods can become adulterated. In other words, the line between adulterated and acceptable moves in both directions.

Since an increased variety of things to eat is a sign of modernization, most of that movement across societies has been towards acceptance rather than exclusion. For example, the lawyer Denis Stearns explains one popular strategy for making food with many chemical additives acceptable. 'Unlike any other product,' he writes,

> only food vouches for itself, regardless of maker or manner of making, playing on the preexisting invitation that only food possesses. It is thus not by accident that so much of the modern marketing of food continues to rely on putting a face on the label in the form of an imaginary maker, like an image of Betty Crocker smiling from the box of cake mix.[19]

This is how many food producers choose to narrow the gap between producer and consumer, to restore the trust that had once existed at a time when these two groups were much more likely to know each other directly.

There have, however, been more than a few cases when a particular food has crossed the line in the other direction. Until 2012, the international coffee chain Starbucks used cochineal, a red food dye derived from small South American insects, in many of its drinks. It had been used in foods for centuries and was approved for use in the u.s. by the FDA, but when word of its use grew, the company's CEO decided that Starbucks 'fell short of [its customers'] expectations by using natural cochineal extract as a colorant in four food and two beverage offerings in the United States'.[20] An additive doesn't have to be harmful to be seen as an adulterant, and in this case it seemed unpleasant to enough people that the retailer feared its use would hurt sales.

This kind of reaction helps explain why 'adulteration' is a reductionist term. It focuses only on the components of particular foods rather than the context in which they are created. Plenty of pure, natural foods are hazardous to the long-term health of the people who consume them because they contain harmful substances that arrived there naturally. Plenty of synthetic foods birthed in laboratories are safe to consume. We purchase the foods we want to eat, and what people want from foods has always been changing. Particularly in an era when food supply chains have become global, those changes are inevitably bound to continue. As food has travelled over longer distances and passed through a greater number of steps to reach our plates, we have lost touch with how foods of all kinds are produced and handled. Even if consumers somehow do know where their food comes from, it is difficult for them to know how their food is processed.

Contrary to most observers, the Canadian sociologist Anthony Winson defines much of modern industrial food processing as adulteration. Like the traditionally deceptive practice of substituting in cheaper ingredients without telling consumers, Winson notes that producers lace food with salt, sugar, fat and chemical additives for the same reason that expensive foods get mixed with cheaper ones or beverages get watered down: all these practices cheapen the cost of production for the sake of profit. All these practices compromise the nutritional integrity of the food consumers eat. All these practices are designed to deceive consumers to some degree.[21]

One difference between the deceptions that form the basis of modern food processing and food adulteration is that the first kind are generally welcomed while the latter are not. As long as consumers maintain a degree of self-imposed ignorance with respect to what is actually in their food, it becomes possible to welcome the price and convenience of highly processed foods without worry. Not telling consumers that you are fooling them for the sake of your bottom line is deceptive, but so is listing a chemical preservative or flavour enhancer on the packaging if consumers don't understand its effect upon what they are eating. The other difference between these two kinds of economically motivated adulteration is that one is legal and the other is not.

While some extreme examples of food adulteration have led to mass sickness and even death, the vast majority of food adulterations will go unnoticed and therefore unreported because few consumers will even realize that they have been affected by this practice. Just because a particular additive that some people might consider an adulterant is legal does not mean it should be welcome. Informed consumers can spend their hard-earned money on foods that meet their standards of purity only if they decide what that standard of purity is. That requires the close consideration of several areas of food controversy that may not at first glance seem to be closely related, such as convenience versus safety or authenticity versus price. If enough people come to agree on how these trade-offs should be resolved, both law and culture can change to reflect this new consensus.

Even the least informed consumers among us have expectations about what belongs in the food we eat as well as what doesn't. Yet there are a surprisingly large variety of ways that our expectations about food ingredients can be thwarted. In some cases, modern consumers will need to adapt those expectations to the inherent risk of being part of the global marketplace. In other cases, understanding the whole taxonomy of how our food can fail to meet our expectations can help us work to improve that situation significantly. Informed consumers are more likely to make better choices; they will be less likely to panic and will be able to make decisions about which kinds of adulteration are acceptable to them and which are not.

1
PARTIAL SUBSTITUTIONS

In 1757, an anonymous author (thought to be one Dr Peter Markham) published an article in the London journal the *Critical Review* entitled 'Poison Detected, or Frightful Truths'.[1] The author quotes a doctor's description of the bread sold in London as including 'lime, chalk, alum, [and] the ashes of bones'. Any baker who uses such ingredients, the author writes, deserves 'the most severe and exemplary punishment. His crime is a complication of fraud, treachery, and parricide. He is the worst traitor to his country: he not only poisons his fellow-creatures, but entails torments, diseases, misery, and death upon their posterity.'[2] Because these problems pre-date mass industrialization in Britain by several decades, it should be apparent that this kind of adulteration is more the product of commercial baking than it is of any particular technology.

The easiest way to demonstrate that fact is to note that this practice persists in places at similar levels of economic development to those of England during the 1750s. 'Alum and chalk are sometimes used to whiten the bread,' explained one Pakistani expert on food adulteration in that country in 2017, adding that 'mashed potatoes, sawdust and plaster of Paris were also used to increase the weight of the bread.'[3] A similar thing was true of milk in the nineteenth-century United States; 'a water shortage would put the milkman out of business,' went one joke from that era.[4]

The principle of these swindles involving bread and milk is exactly the same across the centuries. Substituting ingredients in bread or other foods for cheaper ones reflects the incentive system under capitalism in underdeveloped economies with little regulation, where the potential benefit for would-be swindlers greatly outweighs the risk of detection and punishment. Even honest food manufacturers may feel the need to defraud their customers: if your competitors make substitutions and pass at least some of the cost savings on to their customers, you will be under substantial pressure to do the same or risk going out of business.

If anything, the potential for deceptions of all kinds grows under modern conditions in big cities thanks to the increased physical separation of consumers from producers and the often increasing number of middlemen in the supply chain. Besides substitutions, two related kinds of non-lethal adulteration have become more common as the food-provisioning system has grown increasingly complicated. One involves the addition of small amounts of substances or ingredients designed to mask the inferior quality of the overall food product; this might include something as simple as packing a product in unnecessary ice to increase its overall weight or to water down the product by the time that customers consume it. This sometimes happens to raw fish, for example. The second kind involves food producers removing valuable constituent parts of a product so that other producers can use them – one example would be taking milk solids out of the natural product and selling them separately.[5]

Of course, bread and milk are far from the only kinds of food that can be adulterated in this historic way. Everything from spices to ground beef can be mixed with cheaper alternatives that are difficult to detect, in order to save producers money. Any liquid can be watered down. Anything sold by weight can be short-weighted. Because profit margins in the food business are often so slight, substituting in even a very small amount of cheaper material can provide a great lift to a producer's bottom line.[6] While some of these fillers might have adverse health effects, plenty do not. This may make producers more likely to commit this kind of fraud, since it is not only hard to detect but has relatively few consequences upon its victims, making it less likely to lead to strict punishment.

Separating purely economic adulteration from dangerous economic fraud is an artificial distinction. Nonetheless, one set of problems here builds on the other. Violations of trust occur in both cases, but adulterations that threaten human health are usually easier to detect and far more damaging. This chapter, therefore, focuses on the former aspect: how adulterations threaten the food-provisioning system by violating the public trust. Poisoning (or fear of poisoning), the subject of the next chapter, subsumes many of these same issues. However, that chapter will focus upon the extra problems that these more damaging forms of adulteration create.

Substitutions and Cutting

According to an official working for the Italian Ministry of
Health, the 'vast majority' of food frauds uncovered in the
European Union (EU) involve olive oil. It can be synthesized.
It can be mislabelled. However, the easiest to understand is
the tendency of unscrupulous suppliers to mix inferior-grade
olive oils with more expensive ones, and to then market
the result as a pure version of the expensive, high-grade
kind, thus pocketing a hefty profit. Often, olive oil is mixed
with low-grade, comparatively inexpensive vegetable oil.
Sometimes other kinds of oil, including inferior grades of
olive oil not intended for human consumption, are blended
together in labs. The long supply lines for this product mean
that it can be very hard to identify such adulterations.[7]

Olive oil travels frequently throughout its supply chain.
It is often handled by dishonest wholesalers. Government
officials charged with enforcing its purity, especially in Italy,
often look the other way at olive oil adulteration.[8] The taste of
olive oil varies by region, and in turn varies by the year that
those olives are grown. Olive oil adulteration can destroy the
health benefits that consuming it can bring and add highly
processed oils, and consumers might also be consuming dangerous chemicals with a substance that they thought might
be making them healthier.[9] Since olive oil is a luxury good
and adulterated oils are difficult to detect and expensive to
test, this particular fraud is both common and very lucrative.

The adulteration of dried herbs and spices of all kinds
follows the same principle. Find something – anything
really – that resembles the initial spice and mix it in with

some of the legitimate product: if the match is good it can be impossible to tell the difference even if you taste it. Turmeric is cut with ground corn, nutmeg is cut with cheap pepper, while dried oregano can be cut with plants of all kinds, even weeds.[10] In 2018 a French investigation found problems with half the spices they checked.[11] Another study that same year found that one-third of the spices sold in Canada had been diluted by this kind of substitution.[12]

The most commonly adulterated spice is the one that costs the most. Saffron is the most expensive spice in the world because it is so hard to harvest; the crocuses it comes from are easily damaged and it requires manual labour to remove the stigmata from those flowers, which become saffron threads. This offers a huge incentive to adulterate saffron by dilution or to substitute in its entirety something that looks like saffron threads, even if the substitute requires dyeing.[13] Other parts of the plant itself can be substituted for the tiny threads that make up real saffron. Ground saffron – dried and powdered, as with most other spices – is invariably fraudulent; the easiest way to identify genuine saffron involves the shape of the threads, so grinding makes it extremely easy to mask the fact that the saffron has been cut with other substances.[14]

For all the shock expressed over Britons unknowingly eating an animal that is so beloved to them during the notorious horse meat scandal of 2013, when horse meat was detected in products advertised as being made of beef, this scandal fitted the same traditional pattern: substituting relatively inexpensive components into a more expensive product. Meat from sick horses smuggled into England found its way into highly processed packaged foods because it was much cheaper than actual beef. The fact that the supply chain was long made it easy to obscure the fact that the substitution had been made. Random testing in Ireland and follow-up testing conducted by investigative journalists at *The Guardian* newspaper made this particular substitution known.[15] However, since horse meat is of course in principle safe to eat, the most significant aspect of that scandal remains that it shook people's faith in the idea that they know exactly what they are eating.

Perhaps that faith deserves to be shaken. Meat substitution scandals are surprisingly common. In 1995, a study from the Florida Department of Agriculture found that 16.6 per cent of the meats they tested contained more than 1 per cent of a meat that shouldn't have been present. In 2006, a Turkish study found 22 per cent of meat samples to be adulterated. China, a country with very little regulation, 'has been riddled with meat substitution scandals. There have been reports of rat, mink and fox being transformed into mutton slices.' Adding water to scallops is a common practice that can often be perfectly legal, if the shipper doesn't take it too far. This increases their weight, which in turn increases their price.[16]

To understand the conditions under which these kinds of substitutions occur, it helps to look at the qualities that all of them have in common. For this kind of adulteration to pay off, the food being adulterated has to be expensive. It also helps if the good in question comes in non-discrete units, like spices or ground beef; and substitutions and cutting also become easier when the contributions of individual enterprises are all stored together en masse, like olive oil.

Other common incentives for this kind of fraud include stiff competition within the industry. Competition encourages producers to cut corners if their competitors are doing the same, since if they cannot compete on price they could be put out of business. This becomes more likely if their product is perceived as non-unique – if consumers believe that all olive oil is the same, or don't distinguish between different kinds of ground beef. The bigger the market for a particular food product, the easier it is for unethical actors to slip these kinds of substitutions into at least part of their huge shipments.

Links in the Supply Chain

Historically, the goods that were most likely to be adulterated had the longest supply chains – tea and pepper, for example. Today, however, most foods have long supply chains, and so a much wider range of foods have become susceptible to adulteration, because it is so difficult to oversee their authenticity during their long journeys. When goods are owned by many different parties along the path from producer to consumer, fraud of all kinds becomes more likely. The obscurity of small suppliers in so many global food-provisioning chains makes it harder for both consumers and governments to find who is to blame, assuming their fraud is even recognized.

Honey is a good example of a substance that is apt to be adulterated because it gets handled by so many middlemen. In the European Union, for example, there were 620,000 beekeepers in 2010, and many of these were non-professional.[17] The honey they produce is sold to bulk processors and wholesalers, and sometimes to importers, before reaching retailers and then consumers. Honey labelling requirements vary by country, but somewhere along this long chain much of the honey sold around the world ends up being adulterated. Tests done in 2011 showed that a full 75 per cent of the honey sold in American grocery stores had been adulterated.[18]

Honey, a relatively expensive product, is subject to adulteration with different sweeteners of all kinds. These can include corn sugar, cane sugar, beet sugar and even maple syrup.[19] The filtration of honey is an acceptable manufacturing process as it removes any unwanted sediment, but heat-assisted industrial filtration used at too high a temperature or for too long can change its fundamental composition. Adding water is particularly bad for honey because it brings on fermentation, but since it increases its weight, the practice can still be lucrative for middlemen.[20] Perhaps the easiest and most lucrative adulteration for honey is to mix cheaper honey with a higher-quality product (or to mislabel it altogether).

Even in instances where legal adulterations take place – often by listing any extra ingredients on the label, so that no misrepresentation is occurring – the practice still has disturbing effects. The flavour of honey reflects the landscape in which it was made. Buy industrialized, adulterated honey and the taste will likely be bland and standardized. Nevertheless, plenty of consumers around the world will purchase such honey, because of the low price or the attraction of acquiring large quantities at a lower price. Sadly, they might well be satisfied with that inferior product because the sugars with which that honey has been adulterated are enough to satisfy their desire for sweetness, even if all the geographically generated nuances in the taste of the honey have disappeared.[21]

Yet before we get too carried away with analysing the costs of our globalized food-provisioning system, it is important to remember that it has a primary benefit beyond lowering the price of the final products. Thanks to globalization and the trade that comes with it, people in temperate climes do not have to devote much of their lives to finding and producing foods. Whole regions of the world would be mostly uninhabitable at their current population levels if they could not rely on importing food from elsewhere. Misrepresentation happens, and so do more dangerous forms of adulteration – however, the fact that some products are adulterated should not be blamed entirely on the food-provisioning system, even if the practice of adulteration becomes more likely due to its existence.

Consider the alternative. In order to know exactly what we are eating at all times, we would have to be there when each foodstuff is made. That is logistically impossible. Instead, we are forced to trust that food distributors and manufacturers will not cheat or poison us. Marketing is the primary way that manufacturers try to make this situation tenable; for example, by evoking a traditional method of producing the food in question or a specific place known for making it. Advertising gets consumers to forget about all the links that exist in the provisioning chain before the product reaches them. Since it is a contradiction in terms to romanticize wholesalers and middlemen, their presence is never even acknowledged.

Labelling

Another way that food manufacturers try to instil trust in their customers is through labelling. Assuming that some particular cheaper ingredient is not unhealthy, is it morally acceptable to make a substitution if you announce its presence on the label? This is one of those cultural questions that differs across countries. More information may be welcomed, but whether most consumers will understand or even read the labels of the foods they purchase seems open to question. Legal requirements are only one strand of answers to the question of whether disclosure excuses adulteration. Another strand is the particular expectations across cultures of what belongs in certain foods, and what does not.

Fruit juice, a beverage that would seem self-explanatory, is both prepared and labelled differently around the world. In 1993, a review of legal cases by the *New York Times* found that 10 per cent of the fruit juice sold in the United States had been illegally adulterated – usually with extra sugar or, in the case of orange juice, 'watery orange byproducts'.[22] Both apple and orange juices show up often on lists of foods that are commonly adulterated in North America.[23] Coca-Cola was forced to defend itself against a lawsuit claiming that a drink marketed as 'pomegranate-blueberry' contained only infinitesimal amounts of either fruit. Coca-Cola won.[24] This raises the question of exactly what the word 'adulteration' means to American authorities. The legal contents of any particular juice can be determined in many different ways. While it can sometimes be legal in the United States to sell juice that mostly fails to fit the name on the label, this practice doesn't necessarily make sense.

Most juice in the United States contains a substantial amount of apple juice because that is the cheapest fruit juice available.[25] For example, a 'cranberry juice cocktail' labelled '100% juice' can include grape, apple and pear juice as long as those cheaper additional juices are put on the list of ingredients.[26] The legal logic here is that '100%' refers to the fact that the drink is made entirely of juice, rather than being pure cranberry juice as implied. On the one hand there is definitely a certain amount of deception going on here. On the other, many consumers would likely find pure cranberry juice too bitter or too expensive to drink.[27] Yet if consumers don't find such adulterations unwelcome, they would still be likely to find them unexpected.

The European Union, by comparison, has much more stringent regulations on what can go into fruit juices as well as how they are labelled.[28] Regulations passed in 2012 suggest that 'the composition of the juice should be clearly reflected in the product name'. Under these rules, the cranberry juice cocktail described above would have to be called 'cranberry-grape-apple-pear' cocktail. The new regulations even apply to any pictures that appear on the labels of the bottles or cans: if the same cranberry juice cocktail only had pictures of cranberries on the label, this would not be allowed since it would be likely to mislead customers. These same regulations ban added sugar in fruit juices entirely.[29]

This comparison of fruit juice labelling requirements goes a long way towards establishing the differing cultural priorities of the United States and the European Union when it comes to deceptive food manufacturing and marketing practices. As one olive oil producer said, in summarizing the u.s. Food and Drug Administration's response to fraud in his industry, 'So long as a product isn't toxic, you can sell it however you like . . . It's the consumer's choice whether to buy it or not.'[30] In many ways, this is typical American market-oriented thinking, even though efficient markets depend upon all parties in a transaction being fully informed. Nonetheless, the FDA has limited resources and has thus chosen to concentrate on the kinds of adulterations that pose the greatest risk to health, this being the most efficient way for the agency to use the inadequate funding granted to it by Congress.

China has similar priorities with respect to stopping food adulteration, in this case driven by the fact that the risks that consumers face are greater. One study that determined the percentage breakdown of different types of food adulteration in China found that slightly less than 62 per cent of the cases reported in the Chinese media involved either the distribution of contaminated products or the addition of unapproved ingredients to foods.[31] Because of a series of horrific food safety scares in China over the last fifteen years or so, it makes perfect sense that both the attention and the resources devoted to food provisioning would be used to solve these kinds of problems, at the expense of simple fraud.[32]

The European Union, on the other hand, has devoted more resources towards stopping non-deadly food adulteration in recent years. After the British horse meat scandal, fighting the misrepresentation of food sold in Europe has become a bigger priority in both the EU and many of its member countries. The EU as a whole has worked to understand the possible tools for fighting food fraud in its member states and has begun to gather better statistics about how often food frauds of all kinds occur. In Britain, the approach has moved towards prevention rather than being reactive after some kind of tragedy occurs.[33]

Blends and Mixtures

A partial substitution of any food with a cheaper alternative without telling customers is an adulteration. When you tell customers about a partial substitution of any food with a cheaper alternative it becomes a blend. 'You can't easily proliferate new fruits,' writes Frances Moore Lappé in her classic book *Diet for a Small Planet* (1971). 'If you want endless varieties of colors, flavors and shapes, the answer is more and more processing and ever greater use of food colorings and flavorings.'[34] These are not technically adulterations as long as they are announced, but like adulterations they involve adding something to something else that does not appear there naturally. Even then, consumers still have little understanding of exactly what goes into these blends.

Blended whisky is a classic example of a blend that dates back to the turn of the twentieth century, when distillers developed a way to short-circuit the natural ageing process and create whisky faster. This allowed those producers to sell their product at a lower price than the traditional distillers. In Scotland, for example, blended whisky 'refers to a combination of malt liquors – from different distilleries – built around a base of grain spirit. The resulting liquid tends to be lighter, more approachable, and vastly more popular than its single malt counterparts.'[35] In the United States, blended whiskey has become increasingly popular in recent years since it is usually cheaper than the straight product. Whether consumers understand the difference between whiskies or not, if they like the product then presumably no harm is being done.

Sometimes people will not know that what they're eating is a blend of different foods. Lecithin, for example, is an emulsifier that once came from egg yolk. Now it is usually made from soybeans. Thanks to having taken on this role, soybeans now appear in foods of all kinds – everything from chocolate to margarine. To someone aware of the food science, the soybeans' presence is right there to see on the ingredients list, but most consumers would be shocked to learn that soybeans played such an important role in these common foods. Lecithin is useful to food producers, not consumers.[36] Mixing soybeans into industrial chocolate is not considered an adulteration because there could be no industrial chocolate without soybeans. The consumer will tend to be content with the product, and their reaction is dependent, at least in part, on them not understanding how it is made. How much information a customer requires about such foods is not a legal question but a cultural one. The answers differ both across borders and between different types of food.

You can also blend flavours that don't exist in nature with the help of chemicals, or blend different parts of the same food to create a more consistent, and therefore more market-able, product; this too will change the flavour or in fact may even improve it. While these may be adulterations in the technical sense of that word, they are not the same as other adulterations as long as nobody is being deceived. Perhaps it is best to imagine these activities on a sliding scale from minor beneficial change on one end to deceptive adulteration on the other. The points where a particular change becomes legal and the point where it becomes socially acceptable will vary across different countries and at different times.

Orange juice in its natural state is an incredibly inconsistent product. The taste and smell of different varieties of orange are incredibly diverse. Fruits from higher in the tree are sweeter than those that grow near the bottom. Fruits from the outer parts of the tree are sweeter than fruits from further within. Even which side of the tree the fruit grows on will affect its taste. This is why orange juice is collected in huge vats and then balanced in a laboratory for the purposes of flavour and to promote a consistent taste across a single brand over time.[37] In other words, all commercial orange juice is a blend of orange juices. Even if consumers are unaware of this blending, the fact that it occurs is what makes the product viable.

Analogous to the example of orange juice is ground beef, a blend of meat from many different parts of the cow. Much of it comes from the less expensive parts of the steer in order to keep the cost of the final product down. To make it, a variety of cheap meat from many steers is mixed together and stamped out in uniform units by machines for consistency.[38] If tainted beef makes it all the way to this stage of processing, the result can be a serious threat to public safety. u.s. officials estimate that one disease-infected cow could contaminate as much as 8 tons of ground beef.[39] Hamburger, however, is both convenient and cheap compared to other cuts of beef.

Substitute cheaper meats such as chicken into ground beef and the result will be illegal (unless you label it as such) because it is no longer ground beef. Mix the same meat with fillers like water and soy, list them on the label, and the result is legal, less expensive ground beef. Any manipulation of the product is very difficult to detect visually. Illegal adulteration of ground beef is also very difficult to detect, but the European Food Safety Authority allows for up to 1 per cent of a different meat to be present in ground beef, simply to allow for the inherent sloppiness of running a slaughterhouse, since it can be very difficult to get old meat completely out of the machinery.[40]

Hot dog sausages too are a blend of meats by definition. They often include all the parts of pigs and cows that consumers will not buy separately. They are emulsified into a liquid, water and flavouring is added, and then the resulting substance is poured into artificial casings by machine. In the United States, the home of the hot dog, the parts of animals used in the making of hot dog sausages must now be listed on the label. However, this provision is useless at the baseball games and hot dog stands where so many of them are sold.[41]

Some of these blends are more problematic than others. In 2018, a major American dairy that also produced almond milk accidentally added a single of carton of cow's milk to its almond milk batch, sparking the recall of 150,000 cartons in 28 states.[42] Similarly, Richard Evershed and Nicola Temple, in their important book on food fraud, *Sorting the Beef from the Bull* (2016), note the alarm experienced by UK Muslims, who might consume pork mislabelled as lamb or chicken.[43] Fear of losing customers becomes the main reason that manufacturers admit to blending mistakes and recall their products in response. Again this isn't so much a question of health, but of trust. Regarding food blends, the consumer's expectations of the product are key; in cultures where expectations of purity are low, it is easy to make adulterations of all kinds as long as the taste of the final product is deemed acceptable.

The substitution of inferior but not harmful ingredients does not hurt anybody in itself. However, in places where adulteration is a problem throughout the food supply, adulterated foods will do serious harm if one eats enough of them overall, by denying people the nutrients in legitimate foods. In Bangladesh, for example, malnutrition and disease are common and are often blamed on food adulteration by dishonest producers and middlemen.[44] A lack of healthy, fresh food is one problematic aspect of poverty. In such cases, adulteration is more of a symptom of a poor diet than a cause.

The vast majority of food adulteration and food fraud do not adversely affect food safety, but adulteration can sometimes cause serious illness or death.[45] Causing deaths is, of course, an order of magnitude more serious than simply cheating consumers. However, there is still a long-running intercultural debate about what levels of risk are acceptable when it comes to adding substances to food. Harmful food adulterations that obviously sicken or kill people attract by far the most attention, but it is the grey areas that better reveal the differences between cultures regarding what food is considered to be, and what role it is believed the government should play in its regulation.

2
TAINTED FOODS

In 1968, the *New England Journal of Medicine* printed a letter by Dr Robert Ho Man Kwok of the National Biomedical Research Foundation. It reported that Chinese food gave him headaches. After the letter was published, several other readers wrote to report that they or their close family members had experienced similar reactions. While Dr Kwok listed several possible causes, study of what later came to be called 'Chinese Restaurant Syndrome' focused on monosodium glutamate (MSG). One study showed that huge amounts of monosodium glutamate injected directly under the skin of baby mice caused tumours. As a result, a whole generation of Americans has been scared by a substance that in fact occurs naturally, as glutamic acid (only without an extra sodium ion), in everything from dried mushrooms to soy sauce.[1]

Subsequent research has clearly demonstrated that fear of monosodium glutamate is unjustified.[2] Whatever prejudice exists against MSG does so in spite of that research, and is (as many people have pointed out) influenced by racist attitudes, since plenty of people are willing to consume MSG in Doritos or instant ramen but remain unwilling to cook with it.[3] Meanwhile, MSG is as common as salt or vinegar to chefs and home cooks in China.[4] The cultural context of this ingredient explains some people's headaches better than anything inherent to the chemical compound itself. Ironically, while Americans were once concerned about the presence of MSG in Chinese food served in America, Chinese people are now concerned about the ingredients in the American fast food served in China. Many there consider anything prepared outside the parameters of traditional agricultural practices to be adulterated, whether it originated in the United States or in their home country.[5]

Some additives in the modern food supply are treated like poison even when they are not. Others, meanwhile, are treated like poison because they actually are poisonous. Most of the time it is difficult to tell the difference between these two categories. Arsenic, for example, is a poisonous element that appears in food naturally in very minute amounts. However, it is poisonous in even small quantities. Yet thanks to the industrial use of this chemical, larger amounts are now increasingly common in soil around the world, especially in China. In 2009, the presence of arsenic in plants and in fish led the European Food Safety Authority (EFSA) to lower its provisional tolerable weekly intake levels in 2009; in America, the FDA has changed nothing in response to this.[6]

The key concept needed to differentiate reasonable fear of chemicals in food from unjustified fright is the threshold level of substances needed to cause an adverse health effect upon the people who consume the foods that contain them. For example, a 2018 study by the Environmental Working Group in the United States found that traces of the herbicide glyphosate, used in the weed killer Roundup, had been detected in American breakfast cereals. 'The problem,' writes the journalist Susan Matthews, 'as is always the case when considering toxicity, is dosage.'[7] It is possible to consume small amounts of a poison and survive. Indeed, substances that are technically poisonous at high doses play an important part in the diet of humans. For example, myristicin, found in both nutmeg and parsley, causes headaches if ingested in large enough quantities. The more of these substances you consume, the more dangerous they become.[8]

How much poison you can safely consume depends upon the poison. As Matthews explains it,

> Any substance's potential to cause harm is directly related to how much of said substance you consume; at a high enough dosage, anything can be harmful, and at a low enough dosage, even 'harmful' things can be consumed without *causing* harm. This is why regulatory bodies assess the threshold at which potentially harmful chemicals actually become dangerous and then set regulations for those thresholds.[9]

The threshold for glyphosate as specified by the U.S. Environmental Protection Agency is approximately 140 milligrams per day. The Environmental Working Group found their cereal samples contained about one-hundredth that amount.[10]

In too many cases, the world's press lumps deceptive substitutions in with tainted foods that are acute health hazards when writing about food adulteration. Just because something sounds unpleasant does not mean that it is necessarily dangerous. Talking about the most dangerous forms of adulteration can attract attention to the problem, but amounts are just as important as degrees of toxicity when trying to accurately predict risk. Dangerous food adulterations do occur, but not all food adulterations pose the same level of danger. Separating these instances from legal partial substitutions and the use of food additives is therefore an important step towards understanding the true risk that food adulterations pose.

It has become increasingly easy to slip ingredients that may not be entirely healthy into foods of all sorts. These ingredients might preserve the product in question for longer or make its taste harder for consumers to resist, but if consumers don't understand the long-term health effects of such additives they are in no position to adequately weigh the costs or benefits involved. In the dark about what they are actually eating, consumers will be likely to continue to eat whatever foods appear in their shops.

Food additives serve many important purposes. They can improve the texture of products, enhancing what food scientists call 'mouthfeel'. They can preserve foods, making them last longer. Artificial colours make foods look more appealing, and may prevent foods from changing colour over time. Perhaps most importantly, artificial flavourings make some foods taste 'better'. They can mask tastes that would otherwise make certain foods impossible to eat.[11]

All food contains chemicals. Some of them appear in foods naturally; others do not. The difference between a food additive that consumers consider acceptable – even laudable – and additives that might be considered adulterations again depends on the culture. A society with a healthier attitude towards the food it eats would be more willing to accept the fact that it is impossible to determine whether something is good or bad for you without considering the amount that one is consuming. Where should those thresholds be set? Some societies favour convenience and price over risk. Some countries have legal systems that favour the interests of corporations over the interests of consumers. In some places, consumers eat the limited range of suspect foods that are available to them because they have no other choice. In other places, all these things are the other way around. Which laws are passed and the intensity of their enforcement against even the worst kinds of food adulteration will also vary from culture to culture.

Some cultures value the benefits of most food additives more than they do the risks. Another closely related factor in the acceptance of any additive is a particular culture's tolerance for risk; when there are doubts about the health effects of a particular additive, some cultures will be more accepting of that risk than others. The more conservative that culture is about what should go into its food, the more likely it will be to ban that additive or at least set a very low threshold for its presence in food. There are consumers all over the world who fear chemicals in their food, including sometimes chemicals that appear there naturally. Sometimes those fears are totally unjustified. Sometimes they're not.

Poisons

As food manufacturing has industrialized along with so much else of the world's economy, dangerous industrial chemicals have increasingly found their way into foods. Adulteration that does immediate, visible harm to consumers is of course unwelcome across all cultures. For example, between 2003 and 2005, harmful red dyes were found in spices like paprika across the United Kingdom. This resulted in the largest food recall in the country's history up to that point in time. In 1985, the unwelcome addition of diethylene glycol to Austrian wines practically destroyed the country's wine export industry. Tainted bottles found their way into ten different countries before being recalled.[12]

In 1981, residents in the suburbs of Madrid began going to the hospital with terrible stomach pains. Doctors determined that their symptoms were the result of ingesting cheap cooking oil that had been sold door-to-door in that area as inexpensive olive oil. The oil had been tainted with a toxic agent designed to make it suitable only for industrial uses. This particular batch of oil was eventually traced to French sources. It was mixed with unadulterated oils by a Caledonian middleman. The condition it caused came to be known as Toxic Oil Syndrome (or TOS).[13] This scandal in particular demonstrates a number of traits that many of these kinds of incidents possess: it can be difficult to trace the causes. They are usually international in nature. The total number of affected people can be difficult to determine.

In the TOS case, many perpetrators were arrested and charged, but the exact causes of incidents like these often remain obscure.[14] There have been a few such incidents that were essentially acts of deliberate bioterrorism, but it would be a mistake to assume that all such cases are orchestrated by James Bond-style villains trying to poison millions for the sake of being evil. There have been some fears that terrorists might strike at the food supplies of Western countries, and threats to the safety of food supplies have been received by countries around the world.[15] Very few such incidents have been documented, yet these fears persist throughout the industrialized world.

Deliberate adulteration is far more likely to be the work of international criminal gangs (who have become increasingly involved in food crime in recent years) than terrorists. Their motivation is invariably money rather than creating fear. Luckily, organized criminals seeking profits are more likely to make money adulterating food if they don't kill anyone. These gangs are primarily interested in adulterating the most expensive foods because that is where the most money can be made. In order to be successful, they have to avoid poisoning people, or they risk a huge investigation and increased enforcement in the future.[16]

The problem comes when criminal behaviour designed to make money turns into tragedy; wrongdoers generally know little about the effects of the adulterants they are using and don't always have the resources to understand the risks they are taking when they use potentially dangerous ingredients in their fake foods. A similar situation exists when unknowing farmers use too much pesticide on their crops: residues find their way into the food products they are putting into the supply chain. In both of these situations, whatever quality assurances exist in the supply chain get bypassed. This carries a whole series of mundane food safety risks short of tragedy. However, sometimes the result is a tragedy, with global ramifications for both consumer health and the economic fate of entire industries because the adulteration that took place is not discovered before it has spread throughout a whole web of food chains.[17]

The well-publicized Chinese melamine scandal was originally a case of substitution (water for milk), but became one of poisoning when a particular milk supplier didn't understand the risks they were taking by using melamine to increase the protein level of their watered-down milk. In September 2008, the Chinese government recalled baby formula from one of that country's largest milk producers. The scandal later spread to a total of 22 dairies; some 54,000 children had been sickened because baby formula had been spiked with melamine, an industrial chemical common in glues. Its use in food comes from it being protein-rich, which means it can make already watered-down milk seem more nutritious than it really is. It also causes kidney damage.[18] Six children died as a result of this incident, and 50,000 babies were hospitalized.[19]

People can survive having very small amounts of melamine in their systems. In fact, trace levels of similar substances frequently get into food from certain kinds of packaging. In this instance, however, the melamine in the formula mixed with cyanuric acid (a by-product of melamine production) to form insoluble crystals that in turn caused kidney damage. The same thing had happened in American pet food in 2007.[20]

The complexity of the supply chain for milk in China was a necessary prerequisite for this scandal happening. China experienced something of a milk boom in the decades before the melamine scandal. New dairies spread out of the traditional grasslands in the northern and western parts of the country in an effort to serve the demand generated by the rapidly growing cities on the coast. While there were plenty of modern processing plants in China at that time, they all relied on large networks of small producers to source most of their milk. While this helped the processors meet the varying needs of a growing market, it became much more difficult for those suppliers to check the quality and safety of the product they received.[21]

One of the worst aspects of this Chinese scandal was that the main supplier of tainted milk apparently knew about the presence of melamine in its product for months before acting. It took intervention from that firm's partner in New Zealand for it to understand the potential impact of the additive and to stop production. By then, though, international warnings about other dairy products on the Chinese market that contained melamine had scared consumers all over the world and severely damaged Chinese export markets as a result. One of those affected markets was food aid provided to countries experiencing severe food shortages. Milk sales plummeted in China too.[22] In the long run, no matter how much money a company can make by substituting in cheaper ingredients, the scope of the damage that can be caused by using an adulterant that the company does not fully understand makes this practice bad for everybody involved.

Thanks to globalization, such incidents are by no means restricted to newly industrialized nations like China. In 2005, a food laboratory in Italy informed Britain that chilli powder imported from India had been tainted by the dye Sudan 1, a known carcinogen. While the powder in question had passed through seven different suppliers before reaching the British market, what were then newly introduced European Union regulations about the traceability of foods made it possible to pull the bottles of Worcester sauce to which the powder had been added from British supermarket shelves. Sudan 1 and other illegal dyes have been found in food products ranging from curry powder to palm oil between 2009 and 2012.[23]

Unintentional Poisonings

In a taxonomy of adulterations, human agency matters. While a person who is poisoned intentionally may become just as unwell as one who is poisoned accidentally, understanding why they were poisoned is important for creating policies to prevent such results. To prevent intentional adulteration, the punishment needs to fit the crime. If it is severe enough, it can serve as a deterrent. Yet similar problems can occur as a result of human action for many unintentional reasons. From a consumer standpoint these adulterations are the same, but from a policy standpoint they are very different. To set policies intended to prevent these kinds of adulteration requires the determination of an acceptable level of risk and an inspection regime that will enforce that standard. This can be difficult when food safety problems occur along long, international supply lines. Even when testing occurs, potentially serious problems can be difficult to detect.

Many food safety tragedies are caused by circumstances relating to the natural environment. Such incidents of food contamination have similar effects to deliberate poisoning, even if the causes are not deliberate. This kind of accidental adulteration can be problematic in many kinds of foods. In 2008, for example, Italian buffalo mozzarella makers near Naples suffered a terrible sales drought because of a dioxin scandal. The cause was the local mafia dumping toxic waste; the dioxin leached into the soil, which contaminated the land on which the buffalo grazed, making its way into their milk and eventually the cheese made from it.[24]

Soils that are contaminated with heavy metals (such as arsenic) can leach toxins and taint food at much lower levels without the help of illegal dumping. Many farm crops will extract and store heavy metals from soils. It would be easy to go on describing the presence of a huge array of such chemicals in food, but they are there because enough governments around the world find the risks associated with trace amounts of these substances to be acceptable. Industrial chemicals like dioxin have been discovered in foods all over the world at dangerous levels, however. Polychlorinated biphenyls (or PCBs) are another industrial pollutant that ends up in food in dangerous quantities even though they are not part of the food-making process. The presence of such substances introduces an element of risk to just about every meal that human beings eat.[25]

Fish, especially large, long-living fish like tuna, tend to accumulate toxic heavy metals like mercury that have been dumped into the world's oceans. Eat the fish, and you eat the poisons that they have absorbed.[26] Fish indirectly consume pesticides via the plants they eat.[27] They also consume tiny pieces of plastic that find their way into the sea via pollution or wastewater, mistaking it for food. The problem for human health isn't so much the plastic itself, but the dangerous chemicals that are used in the manufacture of that plastic. It is possible that these toxins could be absorbed into the body of the fish and passed on to the humans who eat it.[28]

Everyday plastics contain chemicals like bisphenol A (BPA) and phthalates. A mounting body of scientific evidence suggests that these substances affect human hormones, which means that their effects on our health are slow, but far-reaching. These potentially dangerous substances can leach into food, especially when food containers made from them are heated. Even if you only store your leftovers in a glass container and don't reheat them in a microwave, avoiding the impact of these chemicals is very difficult: there is a good chance that the food you are eating was stored, lined or heated in plastic before it ever got to you.[29] The effects of substances like these can also be very difficult to assess because they are slow-acting and poorly understood, and it is hard to gauge the risks they pose to consumers around the world.

For all the publicity that incidents of contamination get when they occur, the actual risk of suddenly falling ill from contaminated food in this way is quite low. It's not like what happens when you are bitten by a particularly poisonous snake, or if you're the victim in an Agatha Christie novel. People will seldom die instantly from ingesting toxic ingredients or even industrial poisons. Small doses of hazardous substances do damage over an extended period of time. What separates countries that have strong food safety regulations from those that do not is their tolerance for risk. We all consume minute amounts of poison every day. Countries with strict food safety systems pass laws that help keep those amounts very, very small.

Foodborne illnesses caused by microrganisms are much more acute and more common than illnesses caused by prolonged pesticide exposure. Most foodborne illness leading to hospitalization and death in the United States is caused by improper handling and preparation inside the home rather than in the manufacturing or shipping process. Improper refrigeration, neglecting to wash one's hands, the cross-contamination of foods caused by the failure to wash a cutting board properly: these mistakes at the end of the food provisioning chain are far more likely to make consumers ill than mistakes made at the very beginning, no matter how long the food chain for a product might be.[30]

Dangers of Adulteration in Developing Countries

The cultural anthropologist Harris Solomon tells a story about food processing that went too far for some consumers in India. Puffies are a corn snack sold there that come in plastic bags. Solomon describes how while visiting that country, he heard a rumour that Puffies were actually made of plastic. Indeed, he found numerous videos online of consumers actually burning the snacks in order to 'prove' that they were plastic. For many people, the results led them to believe that the rumour was true. A legal injunction from the multinational company that manufactures Puffies could not put a stop to people repeating the experiment.[31]

Whether Puffies are made of plastic or not is irrelevant to the significance of the protests against them because the flame is symbolic. As Solomon writes, 'The flame illuminates the limitations of thinking elementally to assess bodies with long histories of injuries from unreliable eating. The burn is the refusal to let adulteration happen again. Not plastic, not this time, not for eating. It is not reliable.'[32] The context of living in a society where adulteration is common is essential to understanding the meaning here. Because so many other unwelcome adulterations occur in the Indian food supply, consuming a highly processed, manufactured snack food with no parallel in nature proved simply too much for some people. Everyone in India has to consume water, whether or not it turns out to be dirty. Whether or not one consumes Puffies is a voluntary decision that consumers beleaguered by adulteration were able to use as a point of focus to make a last stand against the practice.

While the Chinese milk scandal suggests the seriousness of the problem of food adulteration in China, strong government regulations helped to limit its lasting effects. The problem in China is that the government is not able to enforce its food safety laws on every one of the many food producers in that huge country before their products enter the stream of commerce. Private companies that buy directly from well-known suppliers help guarantee a steady supply of unadulterated food to people who can afford it. The requirements of servicing a large export market help that situation too.[33] The situation in other developing countries can be much worse, in large part because of the massive informal, small-scale production and marketing of foods.[34] As a result, large segments of these countries' poor are forced to subsist on adulterated food.

It is worth noting that the laws against food adulteration in India are very strict too. But the country is rife with it anyway. In Solomon's assessment, food adulteration in India

> is a daily form of relation between persons, foods, homes, markets and the state. Grain rots in silos, warehouses become labs to tinker with new ways to taint food without notice, ration outlets fail to shake the pebbles out from rice[,] and milk distributors short on supply or long on avarice add water and chalk dust to milk.[35]

Maintaining food safety would be a problem in any difficult conditions, but intentional adulteration is also rampant in India, thereby compounding an already challenging situation. The fact that the government is bad at enforcing its laws has paradoxically made at least some Indian consumers much more aware of exactly what they are eating than those in countries with much more effective anti-adulteration regimes. When you understand the risks of consuming adulterated food because you actually consume adulterated food, you might be less willing to make the cultural shift towards manufactured or fake food products than consumers in countries with safer food supplies.

Similar situations also exist in Bangladesh, Pakistan and other parts of the developing world. In Bangladesh, food adulteration is a problem everywhere that food is sold or produced. This includes food manufacturers, restaurants, food courts and cafeterias, dining halls and fast-food restaurants.[36] Sixty-four per cent of food producers and sellers there reported using chemicals to improve the appearance of their products, to keep them fresher than they would be otherwise or to hold their prices down. They do this despite the fact that 75 per cent of them understood that this practice could harm the health of the people who consumed the foods.[37] In 2014, the Bangladeshi government began a crackdown on using formaldehyde gas to preserve fruit. While the gas can make perishable products last longer, it is a natural carcinogen whose use is illegal in most countries. Its use is also illegal in Bangladesh, yet the levels of this substance found on fruit in that country were over 1,500 times greater than normal background amounts of this substance.[38]

In Pakistan, adulteration is a problem that faces foods including fruit, vegetables, meat and poultry. 'Karachi and Lahore are [the] two largest cities of Pakistan with population [*sic*] of millions of people,' explains one newspaper report on the extent of the problem there. 'Defective and adulterated food products are openly sold in these lucrative markets. The businesses are flourishing and human beings are suffering from all kinds of ill effects and diseases. The consumers have no place to buy pure products.'[39]

Adulteration to these great extents is dangerous both because of the health effects of the substances that get added to food, and because of the fact that the presence of added substances can deny the people consuming these foods the nutrients present in their unadulterated versions. In Bangladesh, adulteration has been found to be part of the reason that 60 per cent of that country's population is malnourished because it affects so many different kinds of food, everything from biscuits to ice cream.[40] This problem falls particularly on children, who have become victims of heart, liver and kidney diseases for reasons tied directly to the adulteration.[41]

Modern chemistry makes adulteration much easier and potentially much more dangerous than even the worst swindles of earlier eras. If such chemical processes are used to adulterate foods in an environment with weak regulation, the results can be far deadlier than in either Europe or the United States. For example, in India turmeric is often coated with toxic lead chromate to enhance its yellow colour. Pesticide residues are common in milk because illiterate farmers cannot read the usage guides, and so do not apply them properly to their crops. Industrial chemicals that are well-regulated elsewhere end up in food grown all over the country because toxic pollutants run forth freely from factories of all kinds.[42]

While it should be possible for almost anyone to detect those forms of adulteration that are visible, modern types of adulteration are particularly difficult to detect if you can't read, because you will be less likely to be able to understand the choices you are making. One study found that Indian women (who do the majority of the food shopping in that country) who were literate were far less likely to buy adulterated food. As the study's authors explained, 'Food labeling is a tool for consumer[s] to make healthy and informed choices which is their right and [it is their] responsibility . . . to read it. But according to one survey only 59% of consumers are able to understand [labels].' Literate women, for example, were far more likely to buy food in sealed packages to hedge against adulteration, thereby making their families less likely to suffer from the ailments it causes.[43]

With so many bad actors and environmental contaminants in the world, it is impossible to reduce the possible risks of eating contaminated, synthesized or adulterated food to nothing. Any clear-eyed assessment would acknowledge that people will inevitably consume certain amounts of toxic substances in their food. The question then becomes how much of these substances is acceptable. The answer to that question will vary by culture. Complete substitutions, or just mislabelling foods, does not vary by culture because lying about what you are selling is never encouraged. What does vary is the level of enforcement brought to bear on those problems.

3
COUNTERFEIT FOODS AND COMPLETE SUBSTITUTIONS

At the beginning of the First World War, the British Navy blockaded Germany, making it very difficult for that country to import many types of food. Faced with shortages, Germans tried to recreate many of their staples with the ingredients they had. For example, they made bread with potatoes. The government certified 837 varieties of substitute sausage. There were 'lamb chops' made out of rice and 'steaks' made from spinach. These new types of food became known as 'ersatz' foods. As the war continued, the substitutions became more and more extreme. For example, by the end of the war, ersatz coffee, which had once been made from chicory root, had become roasted nuts flavoured with coal tar.[1]

Before the war, 'ersatz' foods had meant simply substitute foods, but during the war the term came to be used for foods that were fake and inferior.[2] On one level, this kind of substitution should not count as food fraud. For example, everybody knew that what was being sold as coffee wasn't really coffee, despite the attempt of German propagandists to market their ersatz products as the height of modernity. By the end of the war, the German public was very happy to have access to any kind of food at all. On another, the partial success of these same attempts at marketing ersatz foods – like using jam as a main course – demonstrates how much the German public wanted to be fooled.[3]

These days, the goal is to deceive the consumer by getting them to pay more for something than they would had it been labelled correctly. This kind of swindle tends to originate far up the supply chain, so it becomes hard to hold its perpetrators accountable. These are counterfeits created with the intent to deceive. At other times, a producer's goal is to duplicate the experience of eating the food their product is replacing. This is often done with full disclosure, the replacement marketed as somehow superior. Sometimes, the replacement food is cheaper. At other times, replacements are created because they are said to be healthier to eat than the 'original'.

Some ersatz foods are meant as replacements for foods that appear in nature. Chicory root, for example, was once a popular coffee substitute, but it is now the basis of a welcome beverage in its own right. Should artificial sweeteners be considered fake foods? People drink diet soda instead of real soda to avoid sugar, but in turn often consume far more than they would have otherwise. These goods perform the functions of the originals, but do not depend upon deception for their marketing because their creation does not arise from desperate circumstances. Such highly processed products nonetheless require the same kind of cultural acceptance as ersatz goods once did, and that acceptance should not be taken entirely for granted.

If the ersatz foods of the First World War era fooled nobody, food substitutes of today do a much better job. For example, the American food company JUST, Inc. has created an entirely plant-based mayonnaise. 'My family prefers the flavor of Just Mayo,' explained one *Washington Post* contributor, 'which I think tastes the most like the long-established spreads we know and love.'[4] Yet for a time, the FDA attacked the company for calling the product 'Mayo', arguing that anything that did not contain eggs could not be called mayonnaise. They eventually dropped that argument in favour of demanding a few cursory changes to the label.[5] These quality products might best be considered synthetic foods.

Here again the intent of the producer seems important in understanding whether or not fraud or adulteration is being committed. JUST, Inc. call their product 'Mayo' because it fills the function of mayonnaise, even if it's not actually mayonnaise. Its lack of eggs is actually a big part of its marketing campaign, so many consumers will choose it over mayonnaise precisely because it is different from the original. Like marketable food or flavour blends, this is a welcome substitution – albeit for different motivations. Whether you consider this a new type of mayonnaise, or a new food entirely, depends upon how government agencies classify the product, but it should be immaterial to the consumers who choose to purchase it.

If an ersatz good is something that people understand is intended as a substitute, but is generally inferior to the original, and a synthetic food is an effective substitute, the best term for the categories that remain would be a counterfeit good. A counterfeit good is a good designed to replace another without the consumer's knowledge and may be perfectly legal. Counterfeit foods may not necessarily be unwelcome – wasabi made from horseradish and mustard, for example, since it's so much cheaper than the real thing – if the consumer has no interest in knowing how they are really made. A fake food, on the other hand, could include everything from a cheese puff to the little plastic display foods outside sushi restaurants in Japan that advertise their menus. To dismiss counterfeit foods simply as fake means to fail to examine their wide variety of possible uses.

Similar to foods that are counterfeit, those that are complete substitutions are the replacement of one food with another, done with the intent to deceive. Artificial cheese is a product popular with vegans who don't want to consume dairy products. Label it as such, and it is morally and ethically defensible. However, a 2014 study of takeaway pizza restaurants in Britain found that all twenty of the samples tested were made with this fake cheese. While not illegal, those pizzas should have been labelled as using a cheese substitute.[6] These kinds of counterfeit foods are created to fill a niche in people's diets. They are not necessarily deceptive, but they require that consumers bend their conception of what a food should taste like. Whether they do so wittingly or not should play an important role in determining the ethics of this practice.

Read the ingredients list on a packet of Oreo cookies and you will see that such a product could never appear in nature. Nevertheless, Kati Stephens argues that 'The cookie is not claiming to be anything that it is not. It is not trying to pull a fast one on us. As such, Oreos may be classified as junk food, but they can't be classified as fake food.'[7] However, limiting the discussion of substitutions entirely to deception misses the important cultural ramifications associated with changing tastes in a time of industrialized food production. It is now possible to mix starch, oil and salt, inject the result with food colouring and a sophisticated facsimile of the flavour of avocado, then call the result guacamole.

The flavour industry is built entirely upon these kinds of deceptions. Indeed, the clients of a firm like Givaudan, a Swiss company that builds flavours for clients all over the world, sign confidentiality agreements: sports drink companies and other purveyors of artificial flavourings don't want you to know that the taste of their product is created entirely synthetically.[8] To argue that the presence of any deception is the sole criterion for determining a product's fakeness misses the fact that deception itself is always present in degrees, and that certain kinds of deception are worse than others depending upon the context. By allowing our taste buds to be deceived, consumers around the industrialized world become party to deception. To call this kind of deception an unacceptable adulteration would potentially threaten the legality of many kinds of modern food processing.

Unlike the risk of foods becoming contaminated by pollution, the mislabelling or misbranding of counterfeit foods is clearly the fault of the food producers themselves. If you don't announce the actual identity of your product on your label, then your entire business model depends upon deception. 'There is no food with which we have not interfered before it reaches our hands and mouths,' writes Stevens. 'We have new food but not new thoughts about this food, about the nature of its "reality."'[9] That is only true on an individual level. The context in which people from different cultures see their foods changes, as the way that food is created changes over time. In some cultures, an Oreo cookie or a cheese puff is par for the course. In others, it is an abomination.

Partial Substitutions versus Counterfeit Foods

In 2013, the British government arrested a criminal gang for making counterfeit name-brand vodka. The gang bought bottles from a real distiller, added counterfeit labels and duty stamps, and filled them with a concoction including bleach and methanol. This particular operation produced 165,000 bottles of counterfeit vodka, which denied the British government £1.5 million in tax revenue. While there were no deaths tied directly to this vodka, more than twenty people died in the Czech Republic the previous year from drinking counterfeit liquor.[10] What separates this crime from traditional partial substitutions is that there is no actual vodka in a product that gets its alcohol content from methanol. This crime was a pure fraud.

When partial substitutions and complete substitutions are considered as separate categories of food fraud, the different functions of particular foods become more important in evaluating the ethics of these practices. A food substitute can serve the same purpose as the original even if its taste and components are totally different. Announce its actual ingredients, and a possible counterfeit (like vegan cheese) becomes far more acceptable than a product in which cheaper ingredients have been partially substituted without the consumer's knowledge. Criminality derives from the deception, not from messing with a food in the first place, unless the substitute ingredients are themselves not fit for consumption. On the other hand, the Just Mayo example suggests that labelling your food substitute accurately does not necessarily absolve you of all the responsibility for marketing food substitutes deceptively.

Perhaps the best comparison to this morally acceptable kind of food substitution would be generic drugs. Does a food get the name it deserves because of the ingredients in that food, or do those ingredients perform some kind of higher function, like making your sandwich moist or providing tea flavour to your otherwise boring water? If generic drugs solve your medical problem, you will likely have no qualms if their ingredients are somehow different from the branded alternative. If your artificially flavoured tea quenches your thirst, you will likely feel the same way.

Whether a food is completely fraudulent or merely adulterated depends upon how those foods are made, whether their proper names are used in their marketing, their chemical components or even just whether their place of origin is reported correctly. Many consumers will not recognize or care that they are being deceived if they happen to enjoy the fraudulent product they are consuming. At some point, an ersatz food can become something entirely new and, as was the case with adulterations that became blends, welcome rather than criminal.

As you might imagine, it is harder to create a marketable food product that is completely counterfeit than it is to simply adulterate or water down a legitimate product. A study of food fraud and adulteration incidents reported by the media in China found that only 11 per cent of these events involved foods that were completely counterfeit. This aligns with other estimates, which suggests that these incidents form only a small minority of the total number of incidents of food fraud and adulteration.[11]

However, the range of those counterfeit foods is quite striking. They included ersatz meats, sesame paste, tofu, wine and beer.[12] If a food is particularly easy to fake, it might be counterfeited so frequently that it is very difficult to find an authentic version. Wasabi, for example, is supposed to originate from the stem of the wasabi plant. It is extremely expensive, but it can be easily faked with horseradish, mustard and common food dye. As a result, somewhere between 95 and 99 per cent of the wasabi served in North America is probably counterfeit. Even wasabi that is merely adulterated tends to have only the tiniest percentage of actual wasabi in it.[13]

Other counterfeit foods might resemble the original foods in question, but copy the design of the packaging or the intellectual property of the legitimate producer.[14] Many counterfeit foods get around the problem of packaging by remaining unpackaged, or by fooling the companies near the end of the supply chain that will be doing the packaging. Counterfeit spices are a particularly good example of this kind of fraud. While many are cut with other substances, plenty of the most expensive spices are completely fraudulent. Saffron, for example, can be faked using parts of marigold, carnation or poppy flowers and a variety of dyes, including several that are carcinogenic.[15]

Maple syrup is common, generally sold in bulk (at least up to the point that it gets bottled) and easy to counterfeit. Most of the world's maple syrup comes from Quebec. Cartel-like behaviour by producers there has both raised the price of maple syrup around the world and encouraged unscrupulous producers to fake the real product using sugar and maple flavouring. Real maple syrup is between 66 and 69 per cent sugar and made of maple tree sap. To Canadians, anything else – that is, most processed versions sold in supermarkets around the world – is a fake product.[16] Producers give these products similar-sounding names in order to get around the difference, but are obviously deceptive if you bother to read the label.

Many of the foods already mentioned in this book as frequent subjects of adulteration have also been targets for complete substitution. A combination of sunflower oil, a few drops of chlorophyll, and beta-carotene can make a passable 'olive oil', for example. Honey can be totally replaced by sugar syrup and many consumers won't spot the difference.[17] While fruit juices are easily adulterated, juices marketed as pomegranate juice may contain no pomegranate juice at all because grape juice can be blended in order to make an effective substitute.[18] By one estimate, less than 40 per cent of grated 'Parmesan' cheese in the United States is actually a cheese product at all: whether adulterated or completely counterfeit, the main substitute in this kind of fraud is wood pulp.[19]

Fish Substitutions

It is perhaps logical that the most common form of complete food substitution is fish fraud: there are so many different varieties of fish that it is generally easy to find one that can be mislabelled as belonging to a higher-priced species. The market for fish has a steep hierarchy of prices, making it potentially lucrative to substitute a species for a cheaper one. Substituting one fish for another is also a common practice because few consumers can tell the difference between fishes, and it is especially difficult once a fish has been filleted. Moreover, the supply chains for fish are often long, with multiple links in them, making it increasingly likely that a bad actor willing to defraud consumers will exist somewhere along the line.

Out of 25,000 samples tested across the globe by the environmental group Oceana in 2016, some 20,000 of them were mislabelled. They found mislabelled seafood on every continent except Antarctica. 'Seafood fraud', explain the authors of that study, 'is a serious global problem that undermines honest businesses and fishermen that play by the rules, threatens consumer health, and puts our oceans at risk.'[20] It is difficult to estimate the total amount of economic damage caused by this practice, but this study suggests that by far the most common motivation to commit seafood fraud is financial. In all these ways, seafood fraud is much like most other forms of adulteration.

While many of the most eye-catching stories about seafood fraud highlight the substitutions made at high-end restaurants, fraud can occur at any point in the supply line. And the supply lines for fish are now among the longest for any food product in the world. These lines are often artificially extended when, for example, fish are caught in Alaska and then sent to China for processing, and then returned to the North American market. Fraud is a risk every step of the way.[21] The longer the supply chain, the harder that chain is to monitor. As has been the case with many relatively expensive foods, frauds involving fish can be incredibly lucrative. In 2005, the *New York Times* tested salmon from eight fish stores in New York City and found that six of them had mis-labelled farmed salmon as wild-caught. The price difference added up to about $24 per pound.[22]

The problem of mislabelling also relates to the question of adulteration in that the cheaper seafood that gets substituted for a more expensive variety is often full of toxins. Of the substitute species identified in the Oceana study, 58 per cent carried health risks for the people who ate them.[23] For pregnant women who are trying to avoid mercury, it is important that they know the exact species of fish they are eating in order to make wise choices for their babies' health. Spanish mackerel, which is acceptable in terms of mercury levels, is often substituted with king mackerel, which isn't. U.S. regulations limit the toxins in 'white' canned tuna, but not in 'light' tuna, which can include species of that fish that retain high amounts of mercury. Prawns (shrimp) imported from farms in Southeast Asia are often treated with excessive amounts of antibiotics in order to mitigate the effects of the difficult conditions in which they are raised.[24]

As with so many foods, cultural differences with respect to what to call particular fish are part of the problem. European bass, for example, is also called branzino in North America. Its name in Italian trattorias is *spigola*, while in Portugal its name is *robalo*. Similarly, the name 'moonfish' applies to at least seven different subspecies across the globe.[25] 'Grouper' legally describes 64 different species in the United States.[26] In this environment, it is very difficult for consumers to keep track of the proper names of fish, even if they are used correctly. It is also possible simply to rename a fish, whether because the species is at risk from overfishing or farmed using dangerous chemicals – and it might take a full investigation to rediscover the risks associated with its consumption. This has happened in Brazil, where fish wholesalers invented the name 'douradinha' to provide cover to a particular species of South American catfish that consumers had avoided because of its bottom-feeding habits.[27]

Many of these deceptions can be totally legal. In 2016, an investigation of the American chain Red Lobster found many of their dishes did not contain lobster at all. While a Red Lobster restaurant might display live Maine lobsters in a tank in its lobby, the product you are served will be made with much cheaper langostino.[28] While the name of this creature translates as 'little lobster', it is actually more closely related to a hermit crab. This kind of substitution is technically illegal in the United States unless the crustacean is described as langostino on the menu – but since it is seldom prosecuted, Red Lobster hasn't bothered.[29] Many seafood restaurants in China avoid the risk of such deceptions by bringing the customer the specific fish they have ordered while it is still alive, so that they will recognize it when the same fish appears on their plate with the head still attached.

As difficult as it may seem, there are some seafood frauds that are pulled off with completely ersatz products rather than replacing an expensive fish with a cheaper one. Of the jellyfish sold in Chinese food markets in Italy, for example,

27 per cent turned out to be made of substitutes like bamboo shoots or mustard greens. Fake caviar is a common problem because the potential rewards of faking such an expensive product are so high. A study by German researchers and the World Wildlife Federation found samples that contained no animal DNA whatsoever. What's more, they could not pinpoint the identity of the substitute.[30]

Veggie Burgers, Almond Milk and Cheese Puffs

In May 2018, the state of Missouri passed a bill that banned the representation of non-meat products as meat. The law is aimed at meat substitutes. But these aren't the dry and flavourless veggie burgers of old: the newer, high-tech meat substitutes are so sophisticated they can even 'bleed' beetroot juice when you press down on them while they're cooking. While the legislators who are defending the beef industry in Missouri say they passed the law so that consumers wouldn't be confused, the entire meat substitute industry exists pre-cisely because the products in question are not made from animals, and the people who run these companies aren't shy about advertising this aspect of their products.[31]

Plant-based milk is a similarly booming business in the United States. Soy milk, almond milk and similar beverages have begun to take the place of cow's milk in the diets of many people, either because they prefer not to drink the product of animals or they are worried about the drugs that are injected into American dairy animals, or because they simply want a lower-fat substitute for their usual cow's milk. The U.S. Food and Drug Administration has begun to question whether these products can rightfully call themselves 'milk'. 'An almond', explained the head of that agency at a July 2018 panel discussion, 'doesn't lactate.'[32] Once again, the problem here doesn't come from the fact that customers are being misled. The problem lies in the fact that the producers of one food fear that a new product might perform the same function as theirs, while openly taking a different compositional form.

Like Just Mayo or even the Oreo cookie, these foods are not fooling anybody. They are so-called health foods, designed for people who for whatever reason want to avoid eggs or cow's milk and so on. To over-regulate them based on the idea that consumers might be fooled is particularly ridiculous when other synthetic foods with no basis in nature are unregulated because there is no natural product with which to directly compare them. Counterfeit foods are designed to deceive, knowingly or unknowingly. Foods like Just Mayo are not designed to deceive, yet not knowing what they contain seems like something of a prerequisite for anyone deciding to eat them in the first place.

Consider Cheez Doodles. A Cheez Doodle (a type of cheese puff) is a synthetic product that doesn't mimic the shape or composition of anything that exists naturally. Does it deserve to be considered a 'fake food'? As is the case with so many other processed cheese products available worldwide, it defies easy definition. Federal regulators in the United States have taken to calling the things in which processed cheese appears 'cheese food', 'cheese product' or 'pasteurized processed American', depending on the item, to differentiate it from actual cheese.[33] Wise Foods, the manufacturer of Cheez Doodles, calls them a 'cheese-flavored cheese puff' – something that does not exist in nature.[34] How much more fake can you get than that?

Yet this is precisely its saving grace. Because it is a unique creation, it cannot be argued that it is a substitute for anything else. People who want real cheese will eat real cheese. People who want cheese-flavoured corn snacks will eat Cheez Doodles. The processing that Wise Foods offers makes cheese flavour available to people in a cheap and convenient manner. The Cheez Doodle's strange vivid orange colour is a sign of its synthetic nature and its popularity shows that the people who consume that product don't care how it was made. Cheese puffs are welcomed in some cultures as one of many possible snack foods despite their strange orange colour, while other cultures reject them because they have less interest in products that trumpet the set of values that this product clearly represents.

The sociologist Anthony Winson refers to the ingredients that make these kinds of foods possible as 'macro-adulterants', and he classifies these as 'principally sweeteners, fats and salts'. Although they are not 'acutely toxic poisons', he writes, 'their impact is hardly innocuous'.[35] If there were some kind of cheese puff found in nature, the presence of so many macro-adulterants would lead to outrage throughout the developed world because there would be a clearly natural point of comparison. However, because processed food makers invent new snacks without direct parallels in nature, they maintain the power to set the cultural norms for what kinds of ingredients belong in them and which ingredients do not. As long as synthetic ingredients give rise to products that people actually eat, whether they are found in nature is irrelevant to the people who enjoy them. The same is true of the adverse health effects upon the people who consume them.[36]

In a similar way to how new foods are created using synthetic ingredients, older, existing foods are also being enhanced with a huge variety of natural and artificial flavours. The food writer Mark Schatzker argues that many foods – everything from chicken to bananas – taste more bland and have fewer nutrients than they did just a few decades ago. This is a result of mass production in agriculture: when farmers favour productivity over taste, the dilution of both flavour and nutrients is the inevitable result. Because these mass-produced farm products are replacing nutrients in our diets with more water and more carbohydrates, it seems fair to ask whether these are really the same chickens or bananas any more.[37] What makes these agricultural products even more fake than they might be considered otherwise is the tendency of food producers to add flavours to them so that consumers will not notice their blandness. From burgers and pizza to oats and yoghurt, products on supermarket shelves around the world require added flavour for consumers to find them palatable. Schatzker suggests that all this added flavour – whether natural or artificial – blocks the natural tendency in humans to identify when they feel full, and therefore contributes to obesity.[38] Whether or not you consider the foods that use these flavours 'fake', there is no question they are deceptive. The problem is that many consumers welcome this chance to be deceived.

One particular kind of deception that is rampant (and often legal) in societies around the world is misinformation about where a food product was made. Sometimes producers know they are lying about the point of origin of their products. This is obviously an unethical form of deception. However, in other cases the question revolves around what different societies call particular foods or beverages. These cases do not just require a discussion of what constitutes fraud, it involves asking and answering questions about what particular food products actually are. The difference between a name and the definition of a product bearing that name is sometimes a much bigger discrepancy than you might imagine.

4
THE IMPORTANCE
OF PLACE

During the 1890s the market for sparkling wine, particularly champagne, became very lucrative as newly rich beneficiaries of industrialization around the world wanted to drink the best alcoholic beverages available. However, both winemakers from the French region of Champagne and the peasants who worked for them began to protest the use of the word 'champagne' as a general name for sparkling wines. As residents of Champagne, they understood the unique characteristics of the land where they worked and wanted enough control over the production process to maintain the quality that had always been associated with that name. In 1908, Champagne became the first region of France to receive a designation from the state tying the name of a product to a particular region. By 1935, their region became the only part of France that could legally call its wine 'champagne'.[1]

This did not prevent winemakers in other countries from hijacking the word for use in describing their own products. Today, one American 'champagne' that is made in steel tanks in California sells for about $7 per bottle. Other makers of 'champagne' in the United States use grape varieties that would be prohibited entirely in the French product. The tour guides at Korbel, an old California maker of substitute champagne, incorrectly claim they have a special dispensation from the French government to use the word 'champagne' to describe their product. Not every consumer understands the true origins of Korbel champagne, yet many undoubtedly still appreciate the possibility of toasting special occasions with something that fits their limited budget.[2]

Even if the taste of Korbel pales in comparison to that of any similar beverage produced in France, it remains an open question whether its existence hurts anybody as long as it can still find a market. After all, the two products appeal to consumers in two very distinct income brackets. Moreover, there is only so much champagne that can be produced in Champagne. Korbel helps to both create and satisfy the demand for champagne in the United States. If some Americans don't understand that this 'champagne' isn't made in Champagne, they need only read the label to learn the truth. Compared to other kinds of food fraud and adulteration, this is clearly a step down in terms of the level of deception.

The most serious problem with the existence of cheap champagne involves the erosion of the traditional process of champagne making. The champagne in Champagne is made according to a number of rules that improve its quality compared to the copycat products made elsewhere. It is made almost exclusively from just three kinds of local grapes, and a series of exacting regulations dictate how those grapes can be grown and harvested. In fact, the grapes that go into actual champagne must all be picked by hand to ensure that they are not damaged. The varieties of juices that become champagne are also blended prior to ageing according to highly complex rules. During the last six or seven weeks of the ageing process, the champagne bottles are rotated regularly by hand to help collect the sediment at the neck of the bottle.[3] These are processes that took centuries to develop.

Apart from the cultural knowledge that makes champagne from Champagne a superior product, it also has the benefit of the regional *terroir*.[4] Terroir refers to the effect of local soil conditions and other environment factors upon a given crop. The concept was originally used in France for examining wines grown there, but in recent years various artisan producers have applied the term 'terroir' to other foods. Of course, everything from chocolate to sourdough bread is affected in some way by the environment in which it is produced.

When a food is tied to a particular place, it symbolizes not only that place but the culture that created it. The processing practices that created it developed – as was the case with champagne – over the course of centuries. Copies of that food or drink from elsewhere lack that heritage. They also lack the specific regional traits that make that food or drink taste unique. Globalization aids the process of deception here because it brings these unique foods to the world's attention, at the same time opening a market for inferior copies. Globalization also aids in the process of deception through the economic pressure placed on the producers of the original food or drink to lower their standards so that they can compete in world markets, even if it means sacrificing the traits that make their product unique. But foods that are tied to their points of origin are the opposite of synthetic or counterfeit foods in that they can never really be copied or mass produced.

The practice of trying to duplicate foods that cannot really be duplicated may not be as dangerous as adding harmful ingredients or as deceitful as peddling entirely fake food, but it is deceptive nonetheless. If they don't disclose or brazenly lie about where a copycat food is being made, producers can make money because of the price difference between the cost of their product and the premium that the original, specially designated item can bring. Even if the mislabelled product is somehow comparable to the original, this kind of food fraud harms the unique cultural heritage that accompanies so many of these foods and promotes a homogenization of tastes in which the particular characteristics arising from terroir become less marketable. Moreover, if this kind of misrepresentation becomes normalized, consumers will gradually forget what the original foods taste like. This is a problem not only for the home region and country of a unique food product, but for the consumers, as this kind of fraud will make it harder for the makers of that food to establish themselves and promote their product to consumers elsewhere in the world.

Point of Origin Fraud

Imagine two products that are chemically identical – say, two bars of chocolate. One of them is sourced from a particular place that is known for its chocolate and made in a traditional way. The other was essentially composed in a lab. They are labelled correctly (in other words, differently), but they satisfy the same demand for high-quality chocolate on the world market. Is this a bad thing?

Point of origin fraud is a particular kind of product mis-labelling. Sometimes it is illegal, but at other times it isn't. Nevertheless, if the claim on a label about that product's point of origin is misleading, norms and possibly laws are still being violated. The globalization of food procurement has made just about any food accessible anywhere in the world to people who have enough money to pay for it. As a result, criminals have begun to exploit the ignorance of some consumers about how particular luxury foods should taste.

Since wine can be so expensive, and that expense depends so much upon where the wine originated, many wines besides champagne have been subject to point of origin fraud. In 2002, authorities in the Bordeaux region of France found that many producers were importing cheaper wines from other regions, slapping a Bordeaux label on them, then pocketing the price difference.[5] The origins of the most expensive wines – those with historical significance that are sold by the bottle – were faked so often during the first decade of this century that many super-rich buyers have lost faith in the market entirely. Only recently has that market begun to recover.[6]

As we have seen, olive oil is often trans-shipped from other countries and misleadingly labelled as it is handled by numerous middlemen along the way. Phrases like 'packed in Italy' or 'bottled in Italy' can be used to mask an oil that was actually produced in Spain, Greece or Tunisia, then sent to Italy for aggregation and export. This practice deceives the public by exploiting the association in the public mind between Italy and high-quality olive oil, but is perfectly legal. It helps that few people understand what good olive oil should taste like. Of course, trans-shipments of anything would be impossible without the cheap movement around the world of foods of all kinds in the age of globalization. The best defence against inferior, blended olive oil is for consumers to avoid buying oils labelled 'packed in Italy' or 'bottled in Italy' because those phrases are deliberately deceptive.[7]

Like wine and olive oil, the taste of expensive, unprocessed honey is closely tied to the location where the product is produced. Compounds present in the honey – enzymes, vitamins, minerals and amino acids – appear in various combinations in honey from different places. Honey with a lot of these healthy compounds will fetch higher prices. The exact combination of those compounds in any honey will act as a fingerprint for determining where it originated. European requirements force the honey's country of origin (and other aspects denoting the quality of the product) to be specified on the label.[8] This makes point of origin fraud particularly tempting for aspiring honey criminals.

Some of the most expensive honey in the world is manuka honey, from New Zealand and parts of Australia. Praised as 'liquid gold' by one health-conscious celebrity, it is a product that is specific to those regions since the bees there pollinate the native manuka trees, *Leptospermum scoparium*. While only 1,700 tonnes of the product are produced in New Zealand each year, over 10,000 tonnes are sold as 'manuka honey'. That means many customers around the world are buying adulterated manuka honey or, more likely, something entirely different.[9] Because of these justified fears of fraud, the New Zealand government has begun the testing of all exported honey labelled 'manuka' in order to guarantee its authenticity.[10]

Honey will take on the genetic signature of the plants from which the bees that produced it got their pollen, and therefore the honey has a genetic fingerprint that can be checked. Even though honey can vary in the percentages of different sugars and water that it contains, the amounts of these components in a given honey will lie within a limited range defined by its geographic origin. Perform genetic testing on a certain honey, and the bona fides of the components of that honey and the truth of its origins can usually be determined.[11] Unfortunately, these tests are seldom performed because of their high cost. The result is that corrupt honey middlemen continue to thrive.

The value of expensive food products that attract copies from elsewhere is not always entirely wrapped up in the environmental conditions in which they are made. Sometimes it is also tied to the way that they are manufactured in that particular location. Gruyère cheese, to use one of many examples from Larry Olmsted's book *Real Food, Fake Food* (2016), is a hard alpine cheese named after the town of Gruyères in Switzerland. True Gruyère, which has *appellation d'origine protégé* status, is made in certain areas of Switzerland, including Fribourg and Jura, according to a series of painstaking rules that reflect the fact that it has been produced in the same way since the year 1115. Its taste is also a reflection of the bacteria used in its production, and so whether it is even possible to make a true 'Gruyère' elsewhere is a worthwhile question.[12]

American cheesemakers legally copy Swiss Gruyère because the United States government refuses to recognize the role its local Swiss heritage plays in creating that particular cheese. As was the case with champagne, the word itself has been allowed to be co-opted in the United States, with the u.s. Patent and Trademarks Office arguing that 'the existence of seven u.s. cheese manufacturers of gruyère cheese and the widespread generic internet and dictionary usage . . . clearly demonstrates that gruyère has lost its geographical significance and is now viewed as a genus of cheese.'[13] This being outside their jurisdiction, there is nothing Swiss cheesemakers can do about this practice. However, the existence of American gruyère means that more people will be able to afford tasty cheese at a lower price. Indeed, Swiss cheesemakers cannot make nearly enough of their own product to satisfy demand around the world.

Whether gruyère made outside Switzerland is really gruyère, or whether California champagne is really champagne, has become an increasingly difficult question to answer in recent years. 'As the market becomes more global,' explains Emilie Vandecandelaere of the Food and Agriculture Organization of the United Nations, 'it appears that there is more importance given to the differentiation of products linked to their origin, not only for export products, but also for locally marketed products in relation to their competition with imported products.'[14] Globalization stands in direct tension with the existence of unique local food. Luckily for the producers of those historic products, there are legal ways to resist the tide of cheap imitations.

Protecting Local Food in a Global Marketplace

When producers and consumers know each other, or at least exchange goods for cash in a face-to-face setting, adulteration becomes less likely because it is harder to cheat someone you see in person, and especially someone you know.[15] When food provisioning became a global system and these ties began to break down, food adulteration and food fraud became not only possible, but likely. In many ways, deception regarding the point of origin of particular food products has been incorporated into this system more than the other food crimes covered here, because this global system requires a certain level of deception over where food originated in order to operate smoothly.

Much of the beef marketed as Kobe trades off the reputation of a place with which it has no connection. Real Kobe beef originates in the Kobe prefecture of Japan. Like the Gruyère in Switzerland and the champagne in Champagne, it must be produced under a strict set of rules: the meat must be from the Tajima breed of Wagyu cattle and come from one of only 260 certified farms, which are purposely small in order to maximize the flavour of the meat that is available.[16] Unlike so many other cattle bred around the world, the cows are free from added steroids and growth hormones, and they are fed on grain. The resulting highly marbled steaks are as much a product of this regimen as of the genetic make-up of the cattle breed. While there are plenty of places around the world that claim to sell Kobe beef – it is even allegedly available for purchase on Amazon in the United States – very few of them are actually selling true Kobe beef, because it doesn't meet these strict rules.[17]

The Kobe Beef Association in Japan has opened up the Kobe beef market for global consumption. Ten per cent of the admittedly small Kobe beef production in Japan is now earmarked for export. Most of it goes to other countries in Asia, but it is also available in Canada and the United Arab Emirates, and, since a ban on Japanese exports was recently lifted, the United States too. Nine American restaurants are now licensed to sell the real product by the Kobe Beef Association, and that number has been steadily increasing.[18] High-end American restaurants that claim to sell Kobe beef but are not on the list of sellers approved by the Kobe Beef Association are most likely selling beef from another of the Wagyu breeds, which will also be high-quality meat but will not fetch the same premium as Kobe beef.[19]

In 2015, Kobe beef acquired a Geographic Indicator (GI) designation from the Japanese government in an attempt to gain protection from brand incursion in countries that have foods with geographical indications of their own.[20] Geographical indication protection began in the EU in 1992, and spread to varying degrees throughout the rest of the world through the Agreement on Trade-related Aspects of Intellectual Property Rights (TRIPS Agreement), signed in 1994. Today, the EU has a three-tiered system designed to protect the cultural heritage associated with various food products. Non-EU countries can also apply for the same protected statuses, which will then be protected through reciprocal trade agreements. The lowest level of protection is a Traditional Specialities Guaranteed (TSG) label, for foods produced in a particular way for at least thirty years.[21]

Geographical indications are labels placed on products 'that have a specific geographical origin and possess qualities or a reputation that are due to that origin'. They are used primarily on agricultural products and are designed to convey that where the product came from gives it added value.[22] While the link between the product and the region where it originates should be strong, under the rules for GI designation at least one part of the production can occur outside that region.[23] Besides Kobe beef, other foods that have protection include the Lithuanian cheese Liliputas, and Primorska, a Slovenian wine.[24]

The Japanese designation given to Kobe beef is being honoured by the European Union, but not the United States. There is no definition of what 'Kobe' means in the United States.[25] The history of beef consumption in Japan is actually very short, dating only to 1868. As a trademarked product, Kobe beef dates only from 2001. The GI designation given to Kobe beef demonstrates the desire of Japanese ranchers to expand their global presence.[26] Indeed, a global system accompanied by reciprocal trade agreements can foster famous luxury brands like Kobe beef, rather than simply dilute them.

On the other hand, the geographical indication for Colombian coffee has been very successful. Colombian coffee was the first non-European product to receive a GI label back in 2007. In the United States and Canada, Colombia registered the word 'Colombian' as a certification mark that they could protect. These designations followed a long campaign to promote consumer awareness of the relationship between the coffee-growing conditions in Colombia and the quality of the resulting coffee. The best-known artefact of that campaign remains the fictional coffee grower 'Juan Valdez', used in advertisements as part of that campaign.[27]

Colombian coffee is now part of a range of products that are linked rhetorically to the environment in that country. Each of them is taking advantage of the idea that there are unique conditions there that make them all good.[28] This kind of marketing is exactly how high-quality, locally produced items survive in a globalized food-provisioning system.

Under the EU geographical indication scheme, Protected Designation of Origin (PDO) status denotes foods where the entire production process is associated with the environment and culture of a particular region. Among the products that have this protection are French Bordeaux wine and Greek Manouri cheese.[29] The idea behind this labelling system is to protect regional food production and inform customers of a product's authenticity. By seeing the PDO label, you know that the product really comes from the place that it says it does. This should also, at least in theory, make it less likely for consumers around the world to buy cheap knock-offs – for example of particular high-end varieties of Italian olive oil, or Kobe beef. Many studies indicate that consumers are willing to pay more money for products that carry PDO certification because of their authenticity.[30]

Nonetheless, the United States is under no compulsion to enforce Japan's claim on the name 'Kobe beef'. However, the Japanese beef producers could try to enforce it through lawsuits if they wished. The Japanese government could even try to do this through trade sanctions. Indeed, merely the fear of this kind of action being brought has led to some California sparkling winemakers to shy away from using the term 'champagne'.[31] The EU has tried to enforce its designation that champagne can only come from the Champagne region of France, but while the United States supposedly recognizes the exclusive nature of the term 'champagne', it still permits winemakers who already had that term on their label to continue using it, as long as they note that the wine actually comes from somewhere else.[32]

Like the European Union, the United Nations has its own system for designating foods that deserve protection from creeping cultural homogenization. UNESCO (the United Nations Educational, Scientific and Cultural Organization) keeps a list of what it considers practices and products of Intangible Cultural Heritage, which includes more than a few examples of the world's culinary heritage. Examples include the art of Neapolitan pizza-making and the Mediterranean diet.[33] These, like the rest of the examples on UNESCO's list, constitute 'practices, representations, and expressions, and knowledge and skills which are transmitted from generation to generation and which provide communities and groups with a sense of identity and continuity'.[34] Globalization promotes adulteration, which leads to homogenization that threatens this heritage.

Without any kind of designation assigned to their products, farmers in Norway are banding together to promote their locally produced foods to Norwegian customers. Norway produced most of its own food before the Second World War, but now half of the food calories consumed there come from imported products. In order to maintain the economic viability of Norwegian farming, that country stayed out of the European Union so that it could subsidize its farmers and pass laws like the ones that keep out foreign competition for local crops whenever they are in season. Many Norwegian farmers have begun to market their local products directly to consumers, for example through new farmers' markets, and stress that local food generally tastes better.[35]

'Real foods come from real places,' argues Larry Olmsted. 'When Americans come back from a vacation in Italy and wonder – as they inevitably do – why even the simplest dishes taste so much better there than at Italian restaurants here [in the United States], it is because they have just eaten real food – often for the first time.'[36] This does not mean that the food in the United States is entirely fake or adulterated. It means that the best food has a story that goes with it, and that the industrialization and mass production of food undercuts the importance of that story because it makes it harder to tell. In other words, even if you could duplicate the terroir of the Champagne region, there will always be something special about drinking the beverage made there, in the place where it originated.

The Benefits of Globalization

If there is an opposite of a traditional practice of intangible culinary cultural heritage, it might be industrial salmon farming in Chile. Salmon farms developed there during the 1990s, and they have transformed the economy and culture of southern Chile. Atlantic salmon, kept in pens in vast farms in the Pacific Ocean, are grown to feed the American market, where they are sold at supermarkets at very low prices despite the fact that they were shipped there by air. These farms often pollute the environment and exploit the workers who staff them, but they also form an important component of the Chilean government's view of the country's economic future.[37]

The importance of globalization to adulteration is that it has pulled supply chains across international borders, making it increasingly unlikely that any such deceptions will be caught, let alone prosecuted. Besides making food adulteration harder to detect, globalization has meant that the effects of a single instance of adulteration could spread much further than they would have otherwise. Understanding the nature of food adulteration makes it possible for consumers to recognize the risks posed by this practice. Understanding the differences across cultures in assessing these risks helps explain policy differences across countries.

What a society chooses to grow helps define its cuisine, but the decision to produce very little food is itself culturally determined too. In the early nineteenth century, the economist David Ricardo developed the theory of comparative advantage to explain why particular countries should specialize in the production of particular products. Japan, for example, would have trouble feeding itself on a local diet of rice, potatoes and vegetables if it were not for its ability to trade with other countries.[38] If they specialize in certain products and then trade for other foods, both Japan and the other countries involved will be better off. According to this principle, the same forces that threaten Japan's control over the name 'Kobe beef' benefit that society in countless other ways.

Cultures that favour lower prices or a greater variety of tastes might place less value on the cultural heritage associated with the point of origin of specific foods than on the benefits of having access to, for example, cheap farmed salmon. Despite its homogenizing effects, a globalized food-provisioning system makes it possible for those consumers that have money to buy unique food products shipped in from around the world wherever they happen to be. Such luxury markets help to mitigate the impact of globalization on such goods and ensure demand around the world.

Industrialized food requires a certain amount of homogenization. A pizza chef who cooks using locally grown tomatoes will get tomato sauces that vary in taste, because the taste of those tomatoes varies with the season. The added ingredients in an industrial tomato sauce, on the other hand, help ensure that the taste of the product is the same wherever and whenever somebody opens a jar.[39] If the effects of globalization increase to the extent that it becomes impossible for the makers of unique local products to earn a living, those foods will disappear. Today mass production requires an international market to be sustainable, and any food producer that sells their product around the world contributes something to the homogenization of both the diet and the culture that makes local foods unique.

While the fear that adulteration adversely affects food safety is understandable, the global food-provisioning system is far safer than the system that came before it. Technological developments such as pasteurization, sanitary packaging and refrigeration make it possible to keep food fresh on extremely long journeys, as long as the supply chain has been modernized. So even while the risk of chemical contamination has increased, the decline in the risk from natural pathogens has decreased substantially. Locally grown foods are just as susceptible to bacterial outbreaks, for example, as globally produced ones are – as a particularly bad outbreak of listeria from melons in southern Colorado in 2011 clearly indicates.[40]

In order to make decisions about what adulteration is in a globalized world, any changes that are made to food have to be detected. Those societies that worry most about adulterations are the ones most likely to invest resources in discovering them. How to discover them involves a variety of other surprising decisions. These other variables include what levels of risk are considered tolerable, where in the food-provisioning chain parties are willing to look, and what role governments and extra-governmental bodies play in regulating the supply chain and enforcing its laws. The science of food fraud detection has become much more sophisticated in recent years, and will be covered in the next chapter.

5
TESTING

In 1848, the British chemist John Mitchell explained why he was less than optimistic about the ability of science to detect adulteration. 'As chemistry advanced,' he wrote, 'it unfolded new secrets, and opening on the one hand more decided and unequivocal tests for adulterations, it at the same time gave a larger scope for adulterators.' To take one example, scientists in Mitchell's era had no way to detect whether dairymen watered down their milk. The problem they faced was that the 'density of pure milk is variable', so there was no absolute standard that they could compare milk to in order to be absolutely certain that the milk they were examining had been adulterated.[1]

Milk is still a particularly problematic beverage as far as adulteration is concerned because so much can go wrong with it. One recent paper summarized the situation in Pakistan:

> [The middlemen in the milk supply chain] don't maintain proper hygienic conditions during . . . transport, which leads to increase the total viable bacterial count. They also adulterate milk to increase their profit margin [with] several chemicals like urea, starch, flour, cane sugar, vegetable oils, detergents etc. Various

preservatives like formalin and some antibiotics
are also added in milk to increase its shelf life. This
addition decreases the nutritive value of milk. These
adulterants, preservatives and drugs in milk cause very
serious health related problems.[2]

Unlike in Mitchell's time, testing for adulteration has become
easy enough that people can do it in their own homes. In the
case of milk, it is possible to detect adulteration simply by
putting a drop on a slanting surface and examining the trail
it leaves. It is also possible to detect whether milk has been
adulterated with detergent to improve its colour by mixing a
tiny bit with water and examining its lather.[3] Unfortunately,
people in strained circumstances who are seeking nutrition
in any way they can seldom have the knowledge or the
opportunity to closely examine whatever milk happens to
be available to them.

Plenty of tests now exist to determine whether foods
have been adulterated or whether they do not match their
description on the label in some way. The term used to
describe the use of these tools is 'food authentication', and
many different tests exist according to the varying ways in
which foods can be adulterated. Besides the many man-made
problems described thus far, nature itself makes these efforts
particularly complicated. 'There are complexities to authenticating food that are unlike any other sciences,' argues one
recent overview of this subject.

The complexity of profiling a multi-component food
product requires methodologies that are still far from

routine and easy to use and interpret. There is an incredible amount of inherent variation in the same food product produced over the course of a year. Factors such as climatic and environmental conditions and physiology can produce radically differing product composition of what would be considered the same 'food'.[4]

Honey, for example, is predominantly made up of sugar and water. Add a small amount of additional water to the honey and it is difficult for anyone not party to that act to state definitively that the honey has been adulterated.

The easiest way to detect certain food adulterations is visually. This will not work with honey if the amount of added water doesn't change the colour of the final product. In cases like this and with other more subtle forms of adulteration that still have visual effects, qualitative methods can be used to detect more elusive and serious forms of adulteration as well. If you ask investigators to simply answer a short series of yes or no questions about a food in front of them, it becomes possible to significantly narrow down the possible need for further testing to determine whether a sample is authentic. The more questions get asked, the easier it becomes to visually identify more complicated forms of adulteration without further testing.[5]

Of course, many deceptive practices, like dyeing farmed salmon pink, are designed precisely to make that detection harder. If visual clues don't work, you can guess that adulteration has occurred if someone becomes sick or dies after consuming a particular food product. But for both consumers and the businesses that sold the tainted food, detecting the problem at this point is obviously too late. Moreover, once someone eats a possibly tainted food it becomes very hard to test it, since it has usually gone by the time they suspect a problem. Testing for adulteration has to occur earlier in the supply chain in order to be effective. For a product with particularly long supply lines, businesses will need to make sure it gets tested multiple times, since adulteration can occur at any point. Luckily, even a small amount of private testing can have a real effect on food quality because unscrupulous suppliers will be less likely to seek out the business of firms that authenticate the purity of their products.

A society cannot make good decisions about what it means for a food to be adulterated unless people understand exactly what is in their food. Private companies and watchdog organizations do some testing, but the bulk of this responsibility falls upon government regulators. Those regulators are dependent upon the inevitable ups and downs of the budgetary process for being able to do anything to stop food adulteration, and the amounts available to them to spend are often meagre even in the most prosperous times. Governments ultimately have to bear this responsibility because only they can offer the validation necessary to maintain the trust of consumers, who could never be certain what they are eating is safe entirely on their own.[6] New technologies are making it easier to catch food adulteration and food fraud than ever before, assuming interested parties have the incentive to look.

Fingerprinting Tools

In *Sorting the Beef from the Bull*, Richard Evershed and
Nicola Temple describe how foods are adulterated, then
explain the unique problems surrounding the methods
needed to detect those practices. Writing about food fraud
detection in general, they summarize multiple processes
by introducing food fingerprinting as an overarching
principle. 'The detection of rogue foodstuffs, or rogue
ingredients within foodstuffs, relies upon the identification
of a distinguishing physical/biochemical characteristic,'
they write. That is the 'fingerprint'. The fingerprint 'sets the
adulterated foodstuff or ingredient apart from the accepted
characteristic(s) of a given foodstuff or ingredient'. Honey,
for example, even though it is a simple product, has a sugar
content, moisture content, water-insoluble matter content,
electrical conductivity and other factors that combine to
give it distinct chemical traits that can be measured through
scientific testing.[7]

Different foods require different devices to allow those
fingerprints to be read. Without devoting the entire
remainder of this book to describing all the ways to analyse
different kinds of fingerprints, it is still possible to describe
some detection methods in general and then describe at least
a few of the specialized forms that are required to detect
the methods used by adulterers to undermine the integrity
of certain food products. The general idea behind new
detection strategies in the field of food security is to combine
the advanced technologies that can be applied to particular
food samples with information technologies that can suggest

when and where along the supply chain that food should be tested. Even the most sensitive tests cannot detect food fraud and adulteration unless they are actually employed.

Proactive strategies make it possible to employ these increasingly accurate tests more strategically across a wide array of foods that require testing. For example, mass spectrometry generates ions from a chemical sample (in this case, a food sample) and sorts those ions based on their mass-to-charge ratio. This method of examining food resembles the way criminologists read fingerprints, because the result in each case is unique.[8] Mass spectrometry is particularly useful in detecting foodborne illnesses like salmonella, which can harm particularly susceptible people like the elderly even when present at only low levels.[9] One recent study concluded that 'the potential for ambient mass spectrometry to deliver very rapid and reliable detection of food fraud has been demonstrated.'[10]

Raman spectroscopy is a fingerprinting method particularly well suited to examining foods because it can probe the differences between a wide variety of food elements, ranging from solid proteins to ingredients suspended in solutions. It uses a laser to shoot electromagnetic radiation at the sample and measures the way the molecules vibrate to determine the sample's identity.[11] Another popular detection tool, infrared spectroscopy, involves the measurement of how food samples interact with electromagnetic radiation. This technology has the potential for being used in hand-held devices that can be taken out into the wider world so that testing can be both quick and easy. Some of the most effective uses of this technology include detecting bacteria, food ingredient authentication, and checking the safety of milk and dairy products.[12]

DNA testing is the oldest and most definitive way to identify foods, particularly meats and other foods with identifiable proteins. One recent article on this practice explained how it works: 'By collecting small samples of the food and analysing the DNA it contains, and comparing the results to a library of genetic data from samples of known authentic species, we can quickly determine if a product has been wholly substituted or adulterated with another meat or seafood.'[13] When minced (ground) meat is examined, the exact percentages of products that shouldn't be there (like horse meat in Europe or fox meat in China) can be determined.[14] As the database of available genomes grows, the scope and accuracy of this means of identification will only improve. Genomes aside, even just the analysis of proteins can often be enough to identify particular kinds of foods, and the cost of the equipment to do that is much cheaper than full DNA testing.[15]

As this suggests, the problem with all these tests is that they are expensive to deploy, while the resources available to those who want to do the testing are generally limited. Various statistical methods can be employed to help the process along. Chemometrics, for example, involves using data to group samples together by like characteristics in order to limit the number of samples that have to be tested.[16] As one analysis of food fraud in Brazil explained, 'Chemometric techniques coupled with laboratory analysis have proven to be valuable tools for monitoring food fraud and adulterations. These mathematical and statistical methods are being used for handling, interpreting, and predicting chemical data in order to gain the maximum effective information from the analysis.'[17]

Risk management or risk assessment is another data-based strategy that companies and many governments employ to decide what levels of resources they want to commit to stopping food adulteration and food fraud. Sometimes the development of a risk assessment is required by law, and sometimes companies employ this tactic to a greater degree than required by law because they think it makes good business sense. All of this depends on a firm's risk appetite, another cultural factor that can be assessed in part by looking at data. There are a wide range of different assessment tools that firms can employ to help them make decisions regarding resource allocation in preventing or limiting food fraud.

Detecting Substitutions

There are two general approaches to detect food fraud and adulteration regardless of the technology employed. One way is to test whether substances are present in a food that shouldn't be. The other is to test for the absence of something, namely a specific adulterant. The first works whether you know the adulterant or not, and the second depends upon good information about adulterations that have already happened.[18] Because adulterations can occur in different ways, different tests and strategies need to be employed depending upon the context in which the food is produced, transported and sold. Even if the available tests are effective, the producer or other person must recognize which ones to employ based upon the type of adulteration they are facing.

While tests for existing adulterants are generally effective, keeping up with the ever-changing tactics of criminals can be very difficult. If you are screening for a particular adulterant, your methods will not catch new, unknown adulterants.[19] Once one method to detect adulteration has been employed, criminals can develop new adulterations that can serve as a workaround by giving a 'safe' reading in that test even if the food isn't actually pure. This happened during the Chinese melamine scandal. Melamine gave synthetic milk more protein than it would have had otherwise, and since the test employed for milk in China only tested for protein content, nobody detected the adulteration until long after it was too late. The Chinese authorities were using the wrong test for an adulteration that they had yet to encounter. Inevitably, this same dynamic will play out somewhere again as long as the economic incentives for committing food adulteration and food fraud continue.

Substitutions, the oldest and easiest form of adulteration, can be fairly difficult to recognize because there are so many different products that a food can be substituted for when this particular fraud takes place. Spices offer a very good example of the problems in testing because of the many ways they can be adulterated, and their diverse botanical origins also mean that multiple tests are required. For example, spices are often artificially coloured (which is deceptive by definition), but sometimes those colours can also be hazardous to the health of people who consume them. There are also a huge variety of adulterants that get substituted into spices of all kinds, ranging from ground peanut shells to powdered chalk. Other adulterants may completely substitute for the spice in question, as was the case with saffron described earlier.[20] As a result, the number of tests needed to detect adulterations in spices is high.

DNA analysis has successfully been employed to authenticate various herbs and spices, including saffron and black pepper. This method has the advantage of being both fast and relatively cheap. Mass spectrometry has been employed to identify oregano, saffron and turmeric. As is true with many other foods, a combination of spectroscopy and chemometrics has been used to screen shipments of onion powder, garlic and ginger with some success.[21] All of these wave-based tests share the advantage of making it possible to distinguish between the labelled substance and the adulterant, which is a particularly difficult task when the product comes in powdered form.[22]

The complete substitution of one fish for another might at first blush seem easier to detect because it is so brazen, but authenticating fish species carries its own challenges. What makes fish so difficult to identify is that different species can look very similar once they have been filleted. The shape of the head or the size of the fin are no longer there to help with their identification once they have been processed.[23] The usual method for identifying fish species is through DNA testing. One advantage of this is that it doesn't matter where the cells come from, since the DNA should be identical throughout the fish.[24] There is now a hand-held device called Grouper Check, developed at the University of South Florida, which uses DNA testing technology to determine the authenticity of grouper, and it could be a model for future efforts along these same lines.[25]

As is the case with so many different kinds of food fraud, there has been a mixture of government and private efforts to guarantee the authenticity of fish. The European Union now requires the scientific name of the fish to be included on the label of any processed fish products so that there is a standard against which the content can be judged. The United States established a national commission on seafood fraud in 2014 to look for what it deemed to be the best solution to the problem. The real problem, though, is not the tests themselves, but a lack of testing. The United States, for example, inspects only 1 to 2 per cent of its imported fish, and only a small percentage of that will actually be authenticated using DNA testing technology.[26]

Detecting Point of Origin Fraud and Dangerous Adulterations

The country of origin of various kinds of seafood is often obscured by producers as a way to deter people from testing them for chemical residues of the kind often used in high-volume fish farms, where the fish may have been produced.[27] Farmed fish are supposed to be regularly tested for toxins – not just the chemicals used in the farming process, but the bacteria that naturally result from raising so many fish in such close quarters. Mislabelling the fish is a way to avoid that kind of safety testing. Among more acute dangers, toxic puffer fish occasionally appear on the market labelled as other species, posing a risk for anyone who does not know what they are eating, since they would not know to take the necessary precautions in preparing the fish to be able to eat it safely.[28]

Country of origin testing is, in the words of Evershed and Temple, 'one of the most challenging areas of authenticity testing'. It usually requires running a series of tests simultaneously to get the isotope ratios of a number of different elements that are present in the environment where the most favourable version of that product gets made. As more baseline data for environments all over the world becomes available, however, pinpointing the exact point of origin for anything should become easier.[29]

Coffee has become the second most lucrative industry in the world after petroleum. However, there are coffees that taste far better than others, or are grown or produced in ways that make them more exclusive and thus more expensive. This makes those beans targets for fraud. Coffee is often subject to partial substitution, with adulterants ranging from ground peanut shells to cheaper varieties of coffee. The fact that it is also frequently sold in ground, blended form makes it difficult to determine whether a partial substitution has occurred. Yet unlike many other substances, testing cannot accurately reveal whether coffee is entirely coffee since so many common coffee adulterants resemble the coffee bean. However, it can reveal the authenticity of a coffee's origins. The new methods of component analysis described above have successfully been used not only to detect adulterants, but to determine the exact geographic origins of particular coffees.[30]

Since Colombian coffee has received a protected geographical indication designation because of its quality and the cultural heritage that goes into producing it, mass spectrometry and related detection methods have been able to distinguish Colombian coffee from very similar coffees produced in the same region. The effects of precipitation and altitude on the chemical composition of the coffee make these subtle differences perceptible. But compared to this task, distinguishing Colombian coffee from those coffees grown in other parts of the world is a far easier task.[31] Differentiating between like things is hard to do when the adulterant and the more expensive good are similar – and nothing is more similar than two coffees with close (but not identical) geographic origins.

This raises interesting issues about terroir for foods of all kinds. While you might be able to duplicate the products of a specific region so that they are chemically near-identical, the exact location of its origin does not suddenly become irrelevant. Food chemistry is complicated; there may be something chemical in particularly place-sensitive foods that current methods cannot detect. Nevertheless, the tradition that goes with a food being made in a particular place can often be as important as the taste of the food itself. While the foods themselves may differ only slightly at the chemical level, those differences will be responsible for most of the variations in taste between them.[32] These subtleties are exactly what makes good coffee – and good foods in general – as good as they are.

Dangerous adulterations – the intentional or accidental addition of chemicals that threaten the health of the people who consume them – fall under the category of food safety. Testing for microbiological hazards like dangerous bacteria has been an important concern for decades throughout the developed world. Chemical contaminants could be a tool used by terrorists to harm a country's food supply, or they might be the residues of other industrial activities. The problem here is that if interested parties are not testing for the right contaminants, they are unlikely to spot their presence until it is too late. While the food industry cannot test every bit of food it produces, it may need to test more than it does now to make sure the tools employed are effective and up to date.[33]

It is now possible to detect most kinds of food adulteration more effectively than ever before, but employing those tools requires resources. The question is no longer whether adulterated food can be detected, but whether it will be detected. A problem that had once been mostly about whether the science existed to fix it has become a problem of whether such resources will be deployed in a way that make fixing it possible. As Evershed and Temple explain,

> The stark reality is that the scale of food production is so massive that comprehensive routine screening is an impossible task. The best that can currently be achieved is random testing of what amounts to only a tiny fraction of all the food we consume.[34]

How much risk we are willing to tolerate depends upon how much consumers are willing to pay for effectively authenticated products.

Presumably, the cultural preferences of any society with respect to price, convenience, purity and risk will be reflected in their government policies towards food adulteration and food safety. When and what to test are the most obvious questions that policies directed against intentional adulteration have to answer. Governments that value the safety and integrity of their food supplies will invest more resources in preventing this problem from occurring than those that preferentially value other factors, or that have more limited definitions of what constitutes adulteration. Those who invest less in food safety and integrity need to make sure that the resources they do deploy in this area are spent as effectively as possible.

6
POLICY, STRATEGY AND LEGISLATION

During the 1850s, the eminent British medical journal *The Lancet* published a series of studies by the physician Arthur Hill Hassall devoted to the subject of adulterated food and beverages. While this problem had been recognized as early as those exposés on the bread of London published in the 1750s, these studies led to new regulations like the Adulteration of Food and Drink Act of 1860 and the Sale of Food and Drugs Act 1875. Unfortunately these laws, and other laws passed worldwide in their wake, did not end the problem of adulteration.[1] Indeed, it seems likely that no laws passed to end adulteration will ever stop the practice entirely, because even the harshest penalties will not dissuade criminals who see great rewards in the always possible event that their efforts will go undetected by authorities.

In 2014 two Bangladeshi scholars, Sharifa Nasreen and Tahmeed Ahmed, published a study of food adulteration in Dhaka between 1995 and 2011. They found that more than half the food consumed there had been adulterated and that many of those adulterations were dangerous to the people who ate that food. These findings coincide with those of many similar studies about the extent of food adulteration in that country. Perhaps the most striking part of their study of the food adulteration problem in Bangladesh is their list of the laws in that country that regulate food purity. There are nineteen of them, many of which have been revised, presumably in order to keep up with the times. Unfortunately, the enforcement of these laws falls to multiple ministries in the government, each of which have their own food laboratories and do not share necessary information well. The authors of the study suggest that the strict enforcement of a then upcoming piece of food safety legislation would significantly improve the situation.[2]

These problems regarding enforcement are an indicator of the root of the food safety problem in that country. The government in Bangladesh is not in a position to enforce the rules it has in place to prevent adulteration from occurring, and consumers do not have the political clout to demand that the resources be allocated in such a way as to make it stop. However, mobile court raids are a potentially effective means to stop adulteration. A mobile court is one that moves to where the violations are occurring rather than staying in a judicial building and waiting for law enforcement to bring violators to them. While their use can be applied to a wide range of laws, they are particularly important in enforcing food purity laws because they serve as a way to re-establish the trust of consumers in the entire food system.[3]

Nasreen and Ahmed found that the amount of adulterated food in Dhaka decreased when mobile courts were actively testing food for legal compliance, and that this improvement occurred precisely when those courts stepped up their enforcement.[4] A particularly important problem that hobbles food-related law enforcement in Bangladesh is corruption. 'Do you think food adulteration has decreased?' one official quoted by Nasreen and Ahmed asks rhetorically. 'It has decreased only on the surface; things go on underneath. As long as corruption prevails in our country, it will not decrease. The dishonest traders get the information of mobile court raid[s] beforehand through mobile phone.'[5] Four years after a law passed that led that country's highest court to mandate the establishment of mobile food courts, not a single one had been created.[6]

With the development of commerce, protecting the purity and safety of food was one of the first things that governments had to do. It is a crucial function for any government if they want to have a working economy at all, because a poisoned or malnourished workforce cannot support the functions that sustain a tax-paying citizenry. Since food now transcends international borders, protecting its purity has become one of the most important areas for international cooperation. The sharing of strategies is one of these modes of cooperation with respect to food security. When developed nations help less developed nations in this regard, safety can be increased and thus the countries can become potential trade partners. In some countries where the government does an ineffective job in assuring the authenticity of the products in their food supply, private companies can supplement their role.

Perhaps the most effective strategy that any government can take to improve the effectiveness of the food safety laws it wants to enforce is to consolidate their enforcement into a single body. A 2005 study by the Government Accountability Office in the United States found that seven different countries (Canada, Denmark, Germany, Ireland, the Netherlands, New Zealand and the United Kingdom) had all moved to consolidate their food protection efforts into a single body and were already satisfied with the result.[7] In 2015, the UK consolidated all of its efforts towards food safety and against adulteration into a National Food Crime Unit. Among the many jurisdictions in which it operates is at an international level, an absolute necessity in this age where the supply chains for so many different goods cross international borders.[8]

It is not just the laws themselves but the level of enforcement with respect to those laws that is an important factor in determining how severe a nation's adulteration problem might be. The tolerance of a society for corruption is one factor. So is the entire structure of its political system. 'Adulteration is a matter that is inherently politically sensitive,' argues Anthony Winson, 'not only because of the possibility of injury for the consumer, but also because of the vested interests affected by attempts to curtail it.'[9] The easiest thing that those with vested interests can do to restrict the effectiveness of any food law is to limit the punishments handed out under it. If the costs of breaking the law pale in comparison to the potential benefits, most swindlers will keep on breaking it.

Policy Coordination

Coordination between different government agencies charged in some way with dealing with food safety can help to limit the possibility of food being contaminated, because it makes every agency's efforts more effective. Coordination improves the ability of government bodies to detect contamination problems as well as to intervene in order to limit the damage that those problems may cause. Economically motivated adulteration, on the other hand, requires a more proactive response because it usually requires stopping criminals.[10] A proactive response can involve the use of data to make predictions; for example, when the data for the production levels of a particular product stays steady even when the number of products that claim to contain that product increases markedly, this might suggest that adulteration or fraud is occurring. This makes it easier for regulators to decide where to invest their resources by using the detection methods described in the previous chapter.[11]

An international conversation about food safety in recent years has led to an emphasis on risk management from farm to table around the world. Different kinds of adulteration bear different levels of risk in different places. Terrorist poisonings, for example, are a bigger threat in countries that are politically unstable. Career criminals will commit different kinds of adulteration compared to company employees, and therefore impose different levels of risk and require different kinds of responses.

For most incidents, cross-border coordination of food safety checks is absolutely crucial in today's global economy. No country can guarantee that all the food it sells is safe when so much of it is imported. The United Nations has taken on an important role here through its World Health Organization (who). The who has offered risk assessments to both government and private entities to help them improve the quality of foods that cross international borders.[12] To take one particularly important example of its work, in Bangladesh, besides introducing modern risk management techniques into the country, it has helped the government there build institutions so that it can step up enforcement of existing laws, worked to raise awareness of food safety problems among producers, and trained health professionals to be able to provide better treatment for victims.[13]

The *Codex Alimentarius* Commission (CAC), established in 1961 by the United Nations Food and Agriculture Organization (FAO) and joined by the WHO in 1962, has helped set food safety and quality standards for just about every country on earth. These days that organization is more interested in promoting scientific risk assessment for food safety issues. This has helped improve the quality of the response to such issues worldwide.[14] Two of its most important standards for the purposes of determining whether something is adulterated concern food additives and contaminants. The CAC's food additives standards list those food additives deemed to be safe (as determined by the FAO and WHO) and their maximum acceptable amounts. For contaminants, the standards list sets out limits as to the quantities of background chemicals that may end up in foods, including pesticide residues and veterinary drugs.[15] Here, more than anywhere else, is visible a widely recognized, cross-cultural line between adulterated and acceptable.

In 2012 the United States Pharmacopeial Convention (USP), a private non-profit organization, began to develop a database of food fraud that includes records of every food that has been adulterated and with what. It also describes the measures used to detect this kind of fraud. The information comes from sources like trade catalogues and media reports, and it is designed to be data-mined by whoever is interested in making food fraud risk assessments. The frauds covered in its database include both substitutions and dangerous adulterations that make the final food product a health risk.[16] The USP sold their food fraud database to Decernis, a private information technology company, in June 2018. This underscores the role of such databases as private tools for risk assessment rather than instruments of public policy.[17]

However, using databases to make choices about where in a supply chain to test becomes less necessary when suppliers have a better grasp of where the components in their products originate. Traceability is one way of making it easier to combat food fraud as it allows food and food components to be located at every step in the chain. Strict traceability regulations make it less likely that economically motivated adulteration will occur because potential criminals will recognize that they have a greater chance of being caught, and if any kind of adulteration does occur, it becomes easier for interested parties to track down the exact source of the problem.

There are two kinds of traceability. The first is logistics traceability, meaning the ability to track the physical movement of a product. The second kind of traceability is qualitative traceability, which links specific information about the product (like whether or not the food was organically grown) with the movement of the food itself. One popular tracking system is radio frequency identification

(RFID), which has seen wide use by large international conglomerates such as Walmart.[18]

Traceability has been employed by private companies but has also been embraced by governments looking to improve the safety of their food supplies, and has been embraced by the public sector as a requirement for food safety in all areas.[19] In its General Food Law of 2002, the EU's European Commission defined traceability as 'the ability to trace and follow food, feed, and ingredients through all stages of production, processing and distribution'. Having this ability makes it easier to pull adulterated food off the market, and makes it possible to provide consumers with better information about how they can avoid it. The EU requirement obliges suppliers to know the step that precedes them and the step ahead of them in whatever supply chain they operate in.[20] While this does not mean that everyone understands the whole supply chain by themselves, it does become possible to piece that information together in the event of a crisis.

One of the most interesting efforts to make food more traceable is the global Fish Barcode of Life Initiative (FISH-BOL). The main purpose of this effort is to determine and post the DNA sequences of all known fish species onto the World Wide Web. This will help with ichthyological classifications, but once this information is widely available it will also become far easier to both determine and track through DNA barcodes and subsequent testing fish species that are sold to consumers for food. As the website for this initiative explains in its vision statement, 'Given the estimated $200 billion USD annual value of fisheries worldwide, FISH-BOL addresses socially relevant questions concerning market substitution and quota management of commercial fisheries.'[21] This group has already made great progress towards its lofty goals.[22]

In the United States, the Food Safety Modernization Act of 2011 included several provisions designed to make food more traceable. This included a series of recommendations designed to improve the private infrastructure that would make this possible, as well as recommendations regarding infrastructural improvements that would make it easier for companies to suggest and for the FDA to enforce the requirements that do exist. These efforts began with pilot projects, but the idea is for the legal requirements regarding traceability to be developed further as the best systems and methods are found.[23]

Private Sector Strategies and Policies

The next level beyond traceability in the battle to prevent food adulteration is authentication. Food authentication involves technology that can prove that unadulterated food is unadulterated rather than having to test food to see if it has somehow been tainted in any of many possible ways. Like FISH-BOL, one effort has involved trying to develop electronic tags for foods so that they can be authenticated the same way that Swiss banknotes can be tracked. DNA databases are another way that technology might make this possible. If a food matches the item it should from the range of DNA information on file, then it can be cleared for sale. It is hoped that another technology, nuclear magnetic resonance testing, might one day even make it possible to determine whether or not a food is organic, a particularly difficult task since organic and inorganic produce is genetically identical.[24]

The Global Food Safety Initiative (GSFI) is a non-profit foundation created in 2000 by food retailers, manufacturers and other industry actors in order to improve food safety. While the GSFI cannot certify producers, it helps set the benchmarks for food safety that help keep global food provisioning going.[25] The GSFI has been the most significant private food safety effort globally because so many companies follow their guidance, which itself is based on the totality of food regulations worldwide – firms that follow GSFI guidance are then compliant no matter where in the world they happen to sell.[26]

In other places, anti-adulteration efforts led by private companies can help to raise the standards of producers there. Such programmes have been particularly impactful in China, where large international companies have faced serious problems with various types of food adulteration. International retailers have set up their own private inspection systems to keep adulterated food out of their supply chains. Walmart, for example, spent 100 million yuan over three years to beef up its private enforcement efforts after repeated embarrassing incidents. The company has also reduced the number of local Chinese suppliers it uses, especially in the problematic area of meat, and now has two vans that make unannounced store visits to take samples of the products on its shelves, to confirm that no food fraud is taking place.[27]

Ironically, Chinese food standards are actually comparable to those in the United States and other developed countries, but they are often ignored at the earliest levels of the supply chain: growers and initial producers. Without supervision, melamine can make its way into baby formula, and duck meat can be labelled as mutton in Tesco stores in China. In China, producers are encouraged but not mandated to meet goals that would match those on international markets. The country simply has too many very small food businesses to make it possible for the government to guarantee that all its laws get obeyed.[28] Private enforcement of these standards has become an important tool to separate Chinese food products from those of other Asian countries where adulteration affects a much greater percentage of the food supply.

Private efforts to verify the accuracy of food labels and prevent adulteration have become increasingly important around the world in recent years. 'As food authenticity becomes a greater factor in consumer choice,' write Evershed and Temple, 'the food industry will be further motivated to audit its processes and reduce its exposure to food fraud. As consumers, our role is to hold industry accountable.'[29] There is in fact a thriving food authenticity business, ready to work for any food producer that wants to assure its customers' safety and its own integrity. This newly emerging industry now has multiple global players and is at work around the world – everywhere from the United States and the European Union to developing countries with staggeringly severe food adulteration problems.

Australia, which exports a lot of its food products into Asia, has taken a particularly aggressive approach. One dairy firm has developed its own closed supply chain into Asia. The Australian pork industry has begun a process that allows vendors to validate the country, state and even farm where imported products were originally produced. 'Other companies', explains food safety specialist Dr Steve Lapidge, 'are now offering alternative means of product verification based on isotopic ratios, key trace elements, DNA profiles, mass spectrometry, portable spectroscopy and unique associations of metabolomics linked to the bioclimate, water and underlying geology and soils used to produce the foods.'[30]

Just to give one example of an industry regulating itself across international borders, True Source Honey is an effort set up by honey companies in the United States, with cooperation from producers in other countries like Canada and Vietnam, in order to enforce American anti-dumping laws and combat place of origin fraud. Since low-quality, mislabelled honey can undercut the economic viability of ethical producers, members of this organization have set up an infrastructure to assure high standards for quality and traceability, as well as to ensure that their honey is properly labelled. Companies with honey that meets these requirements earn a private certification logo from that organization.[31]

What makes these private efforts necessary is the tendency in recent years by governments of developed countries to cut back on their food safety and food purity enforcement efforts. In Britain, for example, local governments charged with conducting many food enforcement efforts have lost 63 per cent of their staff since 2008.[32] In the United States, the Trump administration's 2018 budget proposal for the Food and Drug Administration suggested cutting $83 million from food safety programmes across that agency.[33] No law can keep the public safe from adulteration or foodborne illness if the agency in charge of its enforcement doesn't have the resources to do so. The amount of resources given to those agencies, and how that compares to the amounts dedicated to other priorities, is a reflection of the government's attitude towards adulteration.

Governmental Attitudes and Policies

Any government confronted with the problem of food adulteration will inevitably prioritize those transgressions that threaten public safety over consumer deception, since public safety is at the very heart of its mission. Governments also tend to focus their enforcement on physical parts of food-provisioning systems like factories or processing facilities, even though adulteration tends to occur outside those fixed areas. Parties involved in fighting food fraud and adulteration have begun to develop more proactive strategies that favour prevention at the source rather than mitigation after an event has already happened. Today there is a general trend towards focusing on fixing structural problems in the supply chain rather than simply trying to limit the impact of any particular event. This requires incorporating insights from criminology and business administration into anti-adulteration efforts of all kinds.[34]

Whenever government gets involved in food production, determining what the law is in the grey areas between adulterated and acceptable can be difficult. Food producers are free to lobby governments to expand the range of chemicals they are permitted to use when processing their products and the amounts that are deemed to be acceptable. Thanks to long, globalized supply chains, producers are invisible to their customers. Customers are likewise invisible to food producers. This means that producers can either break the law or at least skirt the edges of what constitutes adulteration and face very little risk of being held accountable for that behaviour. Regulations meant to prevent adulteration and promote food safety get circumvented because the profit motive is so often accepted as a cultural imperative.[35]

In the United States, the decision making regarding whether or not to approve a given food additive or colouring falls entirely to the FDA, an executive branch agency of the government that has become highly politicized in recent years. 'Because of inherent limitations of science, FDA can never be absolutely certain of the absence of any risk from the use of any substance,' the agency writes in a primer on this subject. 'Therefore, FDA must determine – based on the best science available – if there is a reasonable certainty of no harm to consumers when an additive is used as proposed.' There are also two huge categories of additives that escape this kind of regulation – those already accepted at the passage of the Delaney Clause in 1958, and any substance which the FDA defines as 'generally recognized as safe' (GRAS).[36] Hire even a moderately effective lobbyist to influence the inspection regime in your sector of the food industry, and a food manufacturer can use the loopholes in existing laws to get almost anything into food that is not obviously poisonous.

On the other hand, it is much, much harder to get a new food additive approved in Europe than in the United States. Kraft Macaroni & Cheese, for example, contains the food colourings Yellow 5 and Yellow 6 (E102 and E110 respectively) when produced for the U.S. market; these additives are generally recognized as safe there. For the UK market, the same product is made without those two dyes because of much stricter standards.[37] The EU, even after testing a substance for safety, requires that any new additive also meet a technological need that cannot be met in other ways, that it is not misleading to consumers and that it has a benefit to consumers. Even then, the use of the additive has to be approved by a standing committee, the European Council and the European Parliament. The EU regularly retests previously approved additives in order to see if they still meet the organization's strict safety standards.[38]

In Europe, the entire burden of proof process for dealing with the acceptance of food additives is the opposite of how it works in the United States. Producers who use commercial chemicals have to demonstrate that their product is safe before they can use it, rather than wait for the government to test it after it has already entered the food supply, as is the case in the United States. Plenty of additives – like brominated vegetable oil, for example, which is used to keep citrus-flavoured liquids from separating, or azodicarbona-mide, a whitening agent used in bread – are legal in the United States, but banned in Europe.[39] The culture in the EU is such that they are unwilling to take risks with the health of its citizens for the sake of commerce.

European Union regulations generally set far lower threshold levels for carcinogens and poisons than in the United States. EU food adulteration regulations require the protection of consumers from 'fraudulent or deceptive practices' and 'any other practice which may mislead the consumer'. Individual member states can pass further protections as they see fit.[40] The General Food Law in the EU specifically places an obligation upon actors throughout the food chain to keep their food safe. As the EU web page describing that law explains, it 'ensures a high level of protection of human life and consumers' interests in relation to food, while ensuring the effective functioning of the internal market'.[41]

On the other hand, the United States government is much more willing to take chances with the safety of consumers. Its regulations only require manufacturers to 'conduct a hazard analysis to identify and evaluate . . . known or reasonably foreseeable hazards for each type of food manufactured, processed, packed, or held at your facility to determine whether there are any hazards requiring a preventive control'.[42] As with so many issues in the U.S., the government relies much more on companies to police themselves than is the case in Europe. With respect to seafood, for example, 50 per cent of imported products are marked with an inspector's stamp of approval in the European Union. In 2010, the United States had only 92 full-time inspectors to inspect the 25 million kilograms (56 million lb) of seafood imported into that country annually.[43]

The best explanation for the vast differences in the attitudes towards adulteration in different countries is culture. The amount of risk to its citizens that a government is willing to tolerate is a cultural question. The way governments allocate resources will also be affected by these cultural proclivities. The same is true of their relative interest in innovation. While science can shed some light on what is or is not dangerous and help detect ingredients that do not appear in particular foods naturally, culture is the main determinant in decision making where the science is not definitive. In this way, it helps in the decision regarding exactly what food is supposed to be.

CONCLUSION: ADULTERATION AND CULTURE

Sodium benzoate is used as an ingredient – with a preservative function – in many beverages, margarine, jellies, jams, fruit juices and even pre-prepared salad. It is also used in many pharmaceutical drugs and can even be used as a rust inhibitor for iron.[1] The American consumer watchdog group Center for Science in the Public Interest believes that sodium benzoate and its close cousin, benzoic acid, appear 'safe for most people, though they cause hives, asthma, or other allergic reactions in sensitive individuals'.[2] The European Food Safety Authority, the food safety arm of the European Union, re-evaluated sodium benzoate as a food additive in 2016 and found that 'the available data did not indicate any carcinogenic potential'.[3] However, this has not stopped sodium benzoate from being controversial.

In early 2017 the American fast-casual restaurant chain Panera Bread announced that it had removed artificial ingredients from its menu. These ingredients included food additives like artificial colours, preservatives and sweeteners that were already approved by the Food and Drug Administration, such as sodium nitrate, sodium phosphate and sodium benzoate.[4] By July, the company had begun to call attention to the move on the social media network

Twitter in an effort to attract health-conscious consumers. 'Call us crazy,' the company tweeted about sodium benzoate, 'but we believe if it's in fireworks, it shouldn't be in your food.'[5] Some of the responses to that tweet were absolutely scathing. 'Panera's anti-science fear mongering is ridiculous. I'm never eating there again,' read one. Another read, 'You can make fireworks with sugar, too. Table sugar . . . This is an absurd level of "chemistry is scary" fear tactics. Stop.'[6] This represents the potential for a sea change in America's attitudes towards food additives. Instead of fearing chemical preservatives, at least one segment of the public was willing to take to Twitter to defend them.

Of course, many other Americans remain scared of chemical preservatives. 'If you Google "sodium benzoate," prepare yourself for a firehose of stupidity,' wrote Derek Lowe, a chemist and writer for *Science Magazine* in response to the Panera tweet.

> There's a long list of sites that are convinced that while benzoic acid is a fresh, healthy, natural ingredient . . . sodium benzoate is a devilish industrial chemical that will rot your soul . . . since I know that the great majority of the readers here have a good understanding of acid/base chemistry, you all must be furrowing [your] brows in puzzlement.[7]

The kind of prejudice against 'chemicals' that helped make MSG controversial remains fully in place today.

Still, the mere existence of an argument here is evidence of cultural change. An American fast-casual restaurant is using the absence of chemicals as a selling point because people fear additives that they don't fully understand. Yet at least some Americans know enough about what goes into their food to denounce this tactic as pandering to people's fears. Benzoic acid, a close chemical relative of sodium benzoate, appears naturally in plenty of foods – cranberries, for example. Further, sodium benzoate has not been directly tied to any human deaths because it is non-toxic.[8] As people get used to consuming additives, their presence becomes less controversial – less likely to be viewed as an adulteration. The questions that have yet to be resolved are how much of these naturally occurring chemicals are safe, and for whom. Panera could have made an argument along the lines of, 'Food without sodium benzoate tastes better,' but instead they made a controversial argument because they assumed that it would attract more attention and, in their case, more customers. Over a century into the industrialization of the American food supply, it is still possible to scare people.

The most important mistake that people make when considering the problem of food adulteration is to confuse what is deceptive with what is unhealthy. Keeping foods looking fresh by adding sodium benzoate might be considered deceptive since it artificially extends the life of whatever food product it is in. However, the scientific consensus is quite clear that the practice does not threaten anyone's health (at least in the amounts of the preservative that people are likely to consume by eating a normal amount of processed foods). The direct health threat from adulteration primarily lies elsewhere. To play up fears over additives by casually associating them with more serious adulterations does not serve the interest of consumers. Cultural forces distort the cause of public safety by using the fact that some societies are more susceptible to this kind of argument than others.

The difference between the United States and the European Union on matters like these is revealing. Europeans draw the line between acceptable and unacceptable in a place that deems more practices unacceptable than where that line lies in the United States, because while the United States tends to welcome risk and entrepreneurial experimentation, Europe tends to privilege safety and tradition. However, many Americans remain frightened by the rapid pace of change in what food suppliers are placing on grocery store shelves. Cultural attitudes towards government in general in the United States make this tendency worse.

It is probably true that many consumers in developed countries around the world are too easily scared when it comes to what goes into their food because they tend to think of adulteration as a binary condition: they believe food is either adulterated or it isn't, when in fact there are varying degrees of adulteration and – perhaps more importantly – different degrees of acceptance for this problem. The historian James E. McWilliams cites the British journalist Rob Lyons comparing the popular equation between the terms 'industrialized' and 'processed' with adulteration and the equation of things that appear natural with 'purity'. 'The reality of contemporary food production,' McWilliams argues, 'whether organic or conventional, whether large-scale or small, fails to follow this purified/corrupted script.'[9] Look at the issue of adulteration in this way, and the real debate becomes over what level of adulteration should be acceptable, not how to wipe the problem out entirely. Even the definition of adulteration can be called into question.

Are GMOS an Adulteration?

Unacceptable adulterations can present an immediate, serious danger to consumers. How much risk consumers are willing to accept is a question that requires that societies are fully informed about those risks. Severe food safety incidents are obviously important, but not particularly revealing, as all cultures recognize that poisoning consumers is always unacceptable. This is the big difference between poisonings and most partial substitutions. Situations where the level of risk is unclear are when the cultural differences involved with food adulteration are at their most stark.

Transgenic and genetically modified organisms (or GMOs) became legal in the United States in 1992. The first such food sold under this regulation was the Flavr Savr tomato, which debuted in 1994. The Food and Drug Administration's reasoning for allowing the sale of GM foods was that they were substantially the same as traditional ones.[10] This decision followed a statement by the World Health Organization and the United Nations Food and Agriculture Organization in 1990 that concluded that genetic modifications were 'part of a continuum of modern breeding techniques'. A follow-up statement by the same two organizations in 1996 noted that the safety assessment of any genetically modified (GM) food should be based upon the existence of a substantial equivalence between it and the non-modified version of that food.[11] While this is not definitive as to their safety, it is clear that this conception takes into account ideas relating to adulteration. If two foods are substantially equivalent, there should be no reason not to replace one with another.

Today, GM foods are an important part of the American food supply. As early as 2003, the Grocery Manufacturers Association estimated that parts of genetically modified organisms were present in between 70 and 75 per cent of all the processed foods sold in the United States.[12] Almost all of the corn and soybean crops now grown in the United States have been genetically modified. While opposition remains, plenty of Americans consume such products without knowing it, since it is not compulsory to cite the presence of genetically modified products on food labels in the United States. This is because the government and the companies that make these crops fear that customers will shun them.[13]

For those who are suspicious of the effects of GM foods on human health, as much of the world is, then they are no different from any other slow poison (although no deaths, or even damage, have been directly linked to the consumption of these products). This dynamic explains the response of the U.S. public and much of the rest of the world to the introduction of GM foods into their respective food supplies. One-tenth of the cropland in the world is now devoted to genetically modified plants. In 2013, genetically engineered crops that carry useful traits like insect resistance or herbicide tolerance (which makes it easier to protect them from weeds) were being grown in 28 different countries. However, the land with those GMO crops is mostly restricted to just four countries: the United States, Canada, Brazil and Argentina.[14]

In the United States, it is more likely that most people have forgotten that much of their food has been genetically modified than that they have somehow decided to trust producers. Most GM foods are not labelled, and it is impossible to identify most GM products just by looking at them. When consumers do not know how their food is made or processed, there is no way for them to know that something has been adulterated. Without a full range of information about what foods are genetically engineered, and without understanding the advantages or disadvantages that might accompany a particular kind of engineering, people are likely to assume that GMOs are unnatural and therefore always bad. With no room on labels to explain the merits of genetic engineering to American consumers, they are often left with no information at all.[15]

In Europe there is very little trust in genetically engineered food products, and public pressure has been strong enough to keep most such foods out of the food supply. These cultural differences have important economic effects. As of 2013, the European Union allowed only two kinds of genetically modified crops to be grown there, a form of maize and a breed of potato that has since been taken off the market. Ten individual EU countries have themselves banned that breed of maize, and four have separately banned that potato. Equally importantly, the EU's hostility to GMOs has been copied by other countries around the world, including India, China and much of Africa.[16] In July 2018, the European Court of Justice ruled that crops created by a new gene-editing technique would fall under the same general ban on genetically modified organisms that had prevented this technology from taking off there in the first place.[17]

What is the difference between new gene-editing techniques and GMOS? The plant geneticist Yi Li from the University of Connecticut explains:

Genetically modified refers to plants and animals that have been altered in a way that wouldn't have arisen naturally through evolution. A very obvious example of this involves transferring a gene from one species to another to endow the organism with a new trait – like pest resistance or drought tolerance.

But in our work, we are not cutting and pasting genes from animals or bacteria into plants. We are using genome editing technologies to introduce new plant traits by directly rewriting the plants' genetic code.

This new kind of gene-editing technique is called 'Clustered Regularly Interspaced Short Palindromic Repeats' or CRISPR for short.[18]

Whether consumers will make a distinction between gene-edited plants and plants where new genes are introduced depends upon their ability to get past the adulteration-inspired mindset. It is difficult to argue that something doesn't belong in a food when it is right there when the plant is growing. It seems likely that as genetic modifications become less invasive, genetically modified organisms will become acceptable over time. Plenty of other modifications that might be considered adulterations in some cultures will eventually become acceptable there too if nobody becomes ill as a result of them. Nevertheless, this does not stop large segments of the world's public from worrying about changes to their food practically all of the time.

Obviously, there are many issues with genetically modified organisms besides whether or not they are safe to consume; those are worth a book all by themselves. However, solely with respect to their safety, a scientific consensus has definitely emerged. 'To date,' writes Paul Enriquez in the *North Carolina Journal of Law and Technology*, 'the totality of institutional, governmental, and international organizations, as well as the scientific literature analyzing the safety of GM foods, has concluded that consuming GM-derived foodstuff poses no more a threat to human health than foodstuff derived from conventional breeding methods.'[19] Most European countries ignore that consensus because they have strong enough governments to enforce strict restrictions on what they see as a dangerous adulteration and a potential environmental threat.

The situation with GM foods in India is telling in a different way. As a developing country, India weighs the need for agricultural productivity as more important than any risks GMOs may carry.[20] As a result, its grocery stores are 'inundated' with genetically modified foods, despite a law banning their production or use in that country. Thanks to poor labelling and lax enforcement, foods containing genetically modified organisms are imported into the country and Indian consumers eat them without knowing.[21] The Indian government may not want to risk the health of its citizens, but the economic forces related to globalization have overwhelmed its ability to enforce the laws that reflect its culture.

American attitudes towards GM foods are beginning to become more favourable two decades after they were first introduced into that country's food supply. A recent poll suggested that consumers there are only slightly more uncomfortable with eating genetically modified fruits and vegetables than they are comfortable with it. Although this is far short of widespread acceptance, this is a significant change compared to when they were first introduced.[22] Even in Europe, where anti-GM attitudes remain rife among the public in many countries, farmers are much more supportive of this kind of biotechnology. Surveys have indicated substantial support for the use of various genetically modified crops among farmers in Germany, the Czech Republic, the United Kingdom, Spain, France and Hungary. Real-world marketing experiments in Switzerland have suggested that European consumers will buy GM foods if given the opportunity.[23]

This suggests the possibility of slippage in the opposition to the use of GM foods, which in turn might apply to adulterations of all kinds that are not obviously unhealthy. Combine the fact that the science on the safety of GMOs is quite definitive with the fact that people aren't dying from eating them and it seems easy to imagine what the future might hold. Since new technology makes it possible to edit genes in plants cheaply, quickly and more precisely, it becomes possible to improve flavour and even increase a plant's nutritional value. To lose those advantages because of an irrational fear of genetic modification would be a shame.

Fear of Food

In 1999 a group of children at a Belgian secondary school began to feel sick and complained of stomach problems and headaches, and were taken to hospital. Investigators traced the outbreak to a batch of strange-smelling Coca-Cola. The next day, after Belgian news outlets had covered the story extensively, four more schools reported outbreaks of illness among their children. The authorities pulled every single Coca-Cola product off the shelf in that country in response. It was the largest recall in the company's history.[24] After investigating, the Coca-Cola Company revealed that some of the carbon dioxide at the local bottling facility had been tainted with hydrogen sulphide, resulting in the strange smell. But the amounts were tiny, not nearly enough to cause illness.

In reality, argues the journalist and writer Malcolm Gladwell in his retelling of this story, Belgian consumers had been stricken by fear. In half of the schools struck by illness, four out of five of the children afflicted had not even drunk any Coca-Cola. This kind of incident is known in the medical literature as a mass sociogenic illness (also known as mass hysteria). The fear of adulteration that Belgian school-children experienced caused real symptoms. The foul smell of the sulphur compounds was enough to trigger hysteria among the population of schoolchildren that were near the tainted Coca-Cola, and even in those who didn't drink it at all. However, nobody had actually been poisoned.[25]

This kind of paranoia, which can be found across cultures with modern food supplies, stems from living in a constant state of ignorance about exactly what you're eating. Artificial colours deceive our eyes. Artificial flavours deceive our taste buds. How food smells intricately relates to how it tastes, and science can manipulate our responses to what we eat by modifying this trait too. No wonder people in Belgium and elsewhere fear that they are being poisoned when something is the slightest bit unusual. Nobody knows what's true about their food or what's false anymore.

This is true throughout the world. Over the last few decades, China's food supply has undergone the same kind of industrialization that occurred in Western countries about a hundred years earlier. Beset by a market filled with fraudulent foods, Chinese consumers have begun to favour foreign over domestically manufactured goods because they see them as more trustworthy. As one study found, 'Chinese consumers participating in this research were unable to dis-associate incidents of economically motivated adulteration from food safety risks that, by implication, present potential health risks.'[26] All foods cause fear, whether or not it is for good cause; Chinese consumers have developed coping mechanisms to deal with this situation, but those are not necessarily based upon good science.

The reaction is different for certain other kinds of adulteration. For example, despite the many warnings about fish absorbing toxic chemicals from their environment, per person consumption of fish almost doubled across the world between the 1960s and 2005.[27] This shows that human beings will eat what they want despite the risks, as long as they have the means to acquire those foods. Even when they know about the risks associated with certain foods, plenty of people – even educated people – are perfectly capable of denying that those risks exist. This is particularly true for people who live in cultures where contradictory information is available and opinions are reinforced by like-minded peers. 'A fear of "chemicals" has become a sickness in American food culture,' argues the food historian Sarah Lohman, 'one that defies logic and is based solely on emotion.'[28] A better way to put it would be that Americans have a fear of the additives they know they are consuming but do not understand.

Food producers, whether ethical or not, will always remain one step ahead of consumers when determining what goes into our food. If a culture decides that something is unacceptable, those producers will inevitably come up with something else. Capitalism is a nearly irresistible force in promoting product innovation in the name of profit. Many of those innovations will be deemed adulterations by the cultures into which they will be introduced. But sometimes all it takes for an adulteration to become acceptable is the passage of time. If no deaths are directly linked to a particular innovation, as with GM foods, it becomes acceptable almost by default.

We are afraid of things that don't appear to belong in whatever foods we happen to be eating. There are cooks and food producers who can innovate, convincing consumers to accept those innovations because the results are delicious. When the ingredients aren't visible, it is harder for people to understand why such changes are necessary. Since most members of the general public don't understand chemistry or physiology in depth, these kinds of changes might even seem like a threat to their health. These cultural responses can emerge from a population almost involuntarily, beginning with what seems like a knee-jerk response of disgust that spreads through a population. Because people tend to be more scared of food they are not familiar with, the array of foods available in their area is an influence on that reaction. However, in an increasingly globalized world, culture will likely trump geography as more societies have greater access to a larger variety of foods.

While strong feelings among a population may be irrevocable, cultural decisions within the broad grey area between adulterated and acceptable are subject to outside influence. Market research is a way for companies both to learn whether something will be acceptable to consumers and to figure out how to influence consumers into finding a particular innovation acceptable. When Pizza Hut decided to put mozzarella cheese inside a pizza crust, market research told them that it would be found acceptable. When McDonald's wanted to create a hand-held breakfast sandwich that used pancakes instead of bread, market research revealed that maple-flavoured crystals that melt when heated would be an acceptable substitute for maple syrup.[29] Many fast-food restaurants will tailor their menus to meet the cultural sensibilities of the countries in which they operate. Chains in India, for example, will not serve beef or pork because of the Hindu and Muslim populations there. Conversely, Starbucks branches in Singapore, Japan and Thailand sell Frappuccinos containing pieces of coffee jelly in order to appeal to local tastes;[30] elsewhere in the world, that drink would likely be out of the general public's comfort zone.

In the United States, consumers are willing to pay a premium for food products that are free from artificial additives of any kind. As a result, an increasing number of companies have been trying to make their labels 'clean', limiting the number of strange-sounding ingredients that go into them so that concerned consumers won't be scared off. One company managed to reformulate their product and drop the number of ingredients in one of its frozen dinners from sixty to fifteen.[31] Assuming the additives that were removed were approved for use in food, initiatives such as these might not actually make any significant difference to anyone's health. What they might do is allay people's most irrational fears of food.

Fighting Fear with Knowledge

The culinary historian and food writer Bee Wilson argues that knowledge of what tasty, healthy food is can be a useful way to fight adulteration because it can give consumers a point of reference to be able to recognize adulterated food. According to Wilson, this strategy

> works not just for agrarian societies but for the modern industrial democracies that most of us now live in. It re-engages the consumer with food, thus counteracting the problem of the long chain between producer and eater. Unlike so many of the other ways of fighting food swindlers, it does not stifle pleasure, or unduly heighten fear.[32]

In fact, knowledge can actually allay fears and subdue anger.[33] Unadulterated food generally tastes better; eat good food, and it's probably unadulterated. This isn't a bad rule, but it is hardly foolproof.

To make avoiding adulterated food easier, consumers should also learn the relative risk of eating the chemicals in their food compared to the myriad costs of eating without them. Modern consumers invariably believe their food carries more risk than it does. In truth, there is no absolute certainty as to how much risk anyone faces when they eat anything, and more importantly we must recognize that that risk can never really be eliminated. 'While we fret about pesticides on apples, mercury in tuna and mad cow disease,' explains the historian Rachel Laudan, 'we should remember that ingesting food is, and always has been, inherently dangerous. Many plants contain both toxins and carcinogens, often at levels much higher than any pesticide residues. Grilling and frying add more.'[34] Processing can actually be one way of bring safer and more convenient food to the masses. To eschew this for the sake of some false sense of security would be a mistake.

The suggestion that a food should be pure should be the starting point for any discussion rather than the end. Having a serious argument about which food additives are danger-ous and which are not, or where the acceptable limits lie for substances widely acknowledged to be dangerous, is very difficult when so few people understand the exact nature of the problem that society wants to solve. Anybody interested in purity must still consider which natural chemicals are acceptable in supposedly pure food. How much processing is acceptable in order for a food to remain pure also deserves consideration.

Understanding entire food systems is important because adulteration can be present without leaving any visual cues or strange aftertastes. More importantly, serious problems that are as important as adulteration do not leave obvious signs either. For example, the way that a chicken or a pig is fed has a huge effect upon the appearance and the quality of the resulting meat. The quality of the soil a carrot is grown in will greatly affect the taste of the salad or stew it eventually goes into. Any culture that is afraid of chemicals but uninterested in these facts does not have a healthy attitude towards food. The more we all know about how food is produced, the less likely we will be to live in fear of what we eat. Eating new foods inevitably carries with it some degree of risk. Assessing the real extent of that risk is impossible without good information about what exactly our food contains.

Just because you don't know where your food comes from does not mean you can't find out. The same traceability practices designed to limit the damage from adulteration can help consumers decide whether their food is authentic and whether it represents the kind of values that they want to promote, such as by paying the additional price of an ethical food company's product. The international fast-food giant McDonald's is the latest restaurant chain to try to get on the right side of that line by taking all artificial preservatives out of many of their most popular burgers. Like Panera Bread, many of the additives McDonald's has removed are perfectly acceptable in both the United States and the European Union.[35]

Unlike Panera, McDonald's is making the case that its food tastes better without additives, rather than claiming that additives themselves are bad. As Chris Kempczinski, the President of McDonald's USA, said at the time of this announcement,

> We know quality choices are important to our customers. From switching to 100% fresh beef in our quarter-pound burgers, cooked right when ordered in a majority of our restaurants, to removing artificial preservatives in our Chicken McNuggets, we've made significant strides in evolving the quality of our food – and this latest positive change to our classic burgers is an exciting part of that story.[36]

Of course, the food at McDonald's has other problems besides the presence of additives, but if using taste as the primary criterion for evaluating the food there makes somebody's diet even a bit healthier, then this move is a step in the right direction.

The multitude of issues surrounding the food at McDonald's is an example of why the line between what is adulterated and what is acceptable cannot be drawn without understanding the entire production process. Industrialized ingredients, for example, can hurt the environment. Most notably, they are grown using pesticides and other chemicals that can adulterate other foods. Informed consumers need to understand the effects of additives both upon individual health and upon the health of all the societies affected by the food system that welcomes products with additives in them.

They need to understand the effects of what they eat not just on themselves, but on the environment at large.

Additives and innovations like poisons, or additives that clearly and immediately negatively impact people's health, are adulterations that we should all reject. But deciding whether something should be rejected actually requires an enormous amount of scientific and sociological research. In the grey areas between adulterated and acceptable, we must rely more on inclination than on science to make this call. The complicated cultural and economic relationships that underpin our interactions with the natural world can serve as the best criteria by which to define adulteration in our societies, if we understand them fully. With so many cultures around the world, each valuing different aspects of the foods they eat, this is not such a terrible result.

REFERENCES

INTRODUCTION: A MATTER OF TRUST

1 Stephen Castle and Doreen Carvajal, 'Counterfeit Food More Widespread than Suspected', *New York Times*, 26 June 2013, www.nytimes.com.

2 Renée Johnson, 'Food Fraud and "Economically Motivated Adulteration" of Food and Food Ingredients', Congressional Research Service, 10 January 2014, https://fas.org, p. 3.

3 Laurence Gibbons, 'Food Fraud Costs UK Firms £11bn a Year', *Food Manufacture*, 28 November 2014, www.foodmanufacture. co.uk.

4 David Edwards, '5 Things to Know About Food Fraud', *Refrigerated and Frozen Foods* (March 2015), p. 36.

5 S. M. Solaiman and Abu Noman Mohammad Atahar N. Ali, 'Extensive Food Adulteration in Bangladesh: A Violation of Fundamental Human Rights and the State's Binding Obligations', University of Wollongong Research Online, https://ro.uow.edu. au, 2014.

6 Karen Everstine et al., 'Development of a Hazard Classification Scheme for Substances Used in the Fraudulent Adulteration of Foods', *Journal of Food Protection*, LXXXI/1 (January 2018), pp. 36, 31–2.

7 Jeffrey C. Moore, John Spink and Markus Lipp, 'Development and Application of a Database of Food Ingredient Fraud and Economically Motivated Adulteration from 1980 to 2010', *Journal of Food Science*, LXXVII/4 (April 2012), p. R122.

8 F. Leslie Hart, 'Adulteration of Food Before 1906', *Food Drug Cosmetic Law Journal*, VII/1 (January 1952), pp. 7–8, 5.

9 Francesca Lotta and Joe Bogue, 'Defining Food Fraud in the

Modern Supply Chain', *European Food and Feed Law Review*, x/2 (2015), pp. 116–17.

10 Many experts define economically motivated adulteration as a subset of food fraud in general. I view fraud as a subset of adulteration since adulteration came first and is far more common than outright fraud. Either way, there is a strong tendency in the literature on this subject to look at food adulteration, food fraud and food safety problems as minor variations of the same problem. This tendency obscures much more than it reveals.

11 Moore, Spink and Lipp, 'Development and Application', p. R120.

12 Lotta and Bogue, 'Defining Food Fraud', p. 120.

13 John Spink and Douglas Moyer, 'Backgrounder: Defining the Public Health Threat of Food Fraud', National Center for Food Protection and Defense, 30 April 2011, p. R160.

14 Markus Lipp, 'A Closer Look at Chemical Contamination', *Food Safety Magazine*, August–September 2011, www.foodsafetymagazine.com.

15 Spink and Moyer, 'Backgrounder: Defining the Public Health Threat of Food Fraud', p. 5.

16 Louise Manning and Jan Mei Soon, 'Food Safety, Food Fraud, and Food Defense: A Fast Evolving Literature', *Journal of Food Science*, LXXXI/4 (April 2016), p. R825.

17 Contamination of food by bacteria is perhaps the central food safety issue of our time. While that comes from the natural environment and not all bacteria are harmful, like with adulterations, different societies will accept different levels of risk.

18 For example, another kind of food fraud involves using legitimate food products and packaging but changing the expiration date. Stealing a legitimate food product and selling it as if it had been acquired legally is another form of fraud. Another kind of adulteration involves contamination during the manufacturing process. While the neglect of sanitary conditions might be economically motivated, the damage caused by product recalls or prosecution make these incidents rare in developed countries.

19 Denis W. Stearns, 'A Continuing Plague: Faceless Transactions and the Coincident Rise of Food Adulteration and Legal Regulation of Quality', *Wisconsin Law Review*, CI (2014), p. 434.

20 Aaron Smith, 'Starbucks to Phase Out Bug Extract as Food Dye', https://money.cnn.com, 19 April 2012.

21 Anthony Winson, *The Industrial Diet: The Degradation of Food and the Struggle for Healthy Living* (New York, 2014), pp. 30–31.

1 PARTIAL SUBSTITUTIONS

1   Bee Wilson, *Swindled: From Poison Sweets to Counterfeit Coffee – The Dark History of the Food Cheats* (London, 2008), p. 78.

2   Peter Markham[?], 'Poison Detected, or Frightful Truths', *The Critical Review; or, Annals of Literature*, 4 (October 1757), p. 296.

3   Mansoor Ahmad, 'Profiteers Pushing Pakistan on Verge of Nutritional Crisis', *International News*, 1 October 2017, www.thenews.com.pk.

4   Robert J. Gordon, *The Rise and Fall of American Growth* (Princeton, NJ, 2016), p. 220.

5   Renée Johnson, 'Food Fraud and "Economically Motivated Adulteration" of Food and Food Ingredients', Congressional Research Service, 10 January 2014, https://fas.org, pp. 6–7.

6   Stephen Castle and Doreen Carvajal, 'Counterfeit Food More Widespread than Suspected', *New York Times*, 26 June 2013, www.nytimes.com.

7   Tom Mueller, *Extra Virginity: The Sublime and Scandalous World of Olive Oil* (New York, 2012), pp. 55–6.

8   Ibid., pp. 57–9.

9   Larry Olmsted, *Real Food, Fake Food: Why You Don't Know What You're Eating and What You Can Do About It* (Chapel Hill, NC, 2016), pp. 86–7.

10 Ibid., pp. 263–4.

11 Joseph James Whitworth, 'French Spice Control Finds Issue with Half of Samples', www.foodnavigator.com, 22 June 2018.

12 Levon Sevunts, 'One-third of Spices Sold in Canada Spiked with Fillers, Says Federal Agency', www.rcinet.ca, 12 April 2018.

13 Richard Evershed and Nicola Temple, *Sorting the Beef from the Bull: The Science of Food Fraud Forensics* (New York, 2016), pp. 211–12.

14 Mark Gorissen, 'The Saffron-Question: Real or Fake?', www.conflictfood.com, 6 April 2017.

15 Evershed and Temple, *Sorting the Beef from the Bull*, pp. 151–3.

16 Ibid., pp. 153–4, 131.

17 Marie-Pierre Chauzat et al., 'Demographics of the European Apicultural Industry', *PLoS One*, VIII/11 (2013), p. e79018.

18 Andrew Schneider, 'Tests Show Most Store Honey Isn't Honey', *Food Safety News*, 7 November 2011, www.foodsafetynews.com.

19 Vlasta Pilizota and Nela Nedic Tiban, 'Advances in Honey Adulteration Detection', *Food Safety Magazine* (August/ September 2009), www.foodsafetymagazine.com.

20 Sonia Soares et al., 'A Comprehensive Review on the Main Honey Authentication Issues: Production and Origin', *Comprehensive Reviews in Food Science and Food Safety*, XVI/5 (September 2017), pp. 1079–80.

21 Lucy M. Long, *Honey: A Global History* (London, 2017), p. 134.

22 Diana B. Henriques, '10% of Fruit Juice Sold in U.S. is Not All Juice, Regulators Say', *New York Times*, 31 October 1993, p. A1.

23 Olmsted, *Real Food, Fake Food*, p. 264.

24 Lauren Valkenaar and Saul Perloff, 'Long Legal Battle Ends with Jury Victory for Coca-Cola in Pomegranate Juice Dispute', www.thebrandprotectionblog.com, 5 April 2016.

25 Olmsted, *Real Food, Fake Food*, pp. 265–6.

26 U.S. Department of Health and Human Services, 'A Food Labeling Guide: Guidance for Industry', January 2013, pp. 8–9, www.fda.gov/regulatory-information.

27 Ethan Trex, 'What Does 100% Juice Mean?', www.mentalfloss.com, 2 August 2011.

28 European Parliament, 'Directive 2012/12/EU of the European Parliament and of the Council of 19 April 2012 Amending Council Directive 2001/112/EC Relating to Fruit Juices . . .', http://eur-lex.europa.eu, 27 April 2012.

29 USDA Foreign Agricultural Service, 'New EU Fruit Juice Labeling Rules', http://gain.fas.usda.gov, 31 May 2012.

30 Mueller, *Extra Virginity*, p. 196.

31 Wenjing Zhang and Jianhong Xue, 'Economically Motivated Food Fraud and Adulteration in China: An Analysis Based on 1,553 Media Reports', *Food Control*, LXVII (September 2016), p. 94.

32 Xu Nan, 'A Decade of Food Safety in China', *ChinaDialogue*, 6 August 2012, www.chinadialogue.net.

33 Evershed and Temple, *Sorting the Beef from the Bull*, pp. 39, 35–7.

34 Frances Moore Lappé, *Diet for a Small Planet*, 20th anniversary edn (New York, 1991), p. 147.

35 Brad Japhe, 'For American Whiskies, the Next Big Trend is the Blend', *Forbes*, 8 July 2018, www.forbes.com.
36 Raj Patel, *Stuffed and Starved: Markets, Power and the Hidden Battle for the World's Food System* (London, 2007), p. 166.
37 John McPhee, *Oranges* (New York, 1967), p. 8.
38 Paul Roberts, *The End of Food* (Boston, MA, 2008), p. 73.
39 Marion Nestle, *Safe Food: The Politics of Food Safety*, 2nd edn (Berkeley, CA, 2010), p. 45.
40 Evershed and Temple, *Sorting the Beef from the Bull*, pp. 154–7.
41 Roger Horowitz, *Putting Meat on the American Table: Taste, Technology, Transformation* (Baltimore, MD, 2006), pp. 100–102.
42 Cleve R. Wootson Jr, 'Somebody Added Cow's Milk to Almond Breeze, FDA Says, Sparking a Recall in 28 States', *Washington Post*, 4 August 2018, www.washingtonpost.com.
43 Evershed and Temple, *Sorting the Beef from the Bull*, pp. 19–20.
44 *New Nation* (Bangladesh), 20 March 2015.
45 Johnson, 'Food Fraud and "Economically Motivated Adulteration"', p. 1.

2 TAINTED FOODS

1 Sarah Lohman, *Eight Flavors: The Untold Story of American Cuisine* (New York, 2016), pp. 189–92.
2 Alex Renton, 'If MSG is So Bad For You, Why Doesn't Everyone in Asia Have a Headache?', *The Observer*, 10 July 2005, www.theguardian.com.
3 Helen Rosner, 'An MSG Convert Visits the High Church of Umami', *New Yorker*, 27 April 2018, www.newyorker.com.
4 Fuchsia Dunlop, 'China's True Dash of Flavor', *New York Times*, 18 February 2007, www.nytimes.com.
5 Jerry Tsao, 'A Taste of Culture: Perceptions About American Fast Food in China', unpublished MA thesis, East Carolina University, Greenville, NC (2012), p. 41.
6 Mike Adams, *Food Forensics: The Hidden Toxins Lurking in Your Food and How You Can Avoid Them for Lifelong Health* (Dallas, TX, 2016), pp. 16–32.
7 Susan Matthews, 'You Don't Need to Worry about Roundup in Your Breakfast Cereal', www.slate.com, 16 August 2018.

8 Mark Schatzker, *The Dorito Effect: The Surprising New Truth about Food and Flavor* (New York, 2015), pp. 151–2.

9 Matthews, 'You Don't Need to Worry about Roundup'.

10 Ibid.

11 Melanie Warner, *Pandora's Lunchbox: How Processed Food Took Over the American Meal* (New York, 2013), p. 99.

12 Jeffrey C. Moore, John Spink and Markus Lipp, 'Development and Application of a Database of Food Ingredient Fraud and Economically Motivated Adulteration from 1980 to 2010', *Journal of Food Science*, LXXVII/4 (April 2012), p. R124.

13 Richard Evershed and Nicola Temple, *Sorting the Beef from the Bull: The Science of Food Fraud Forensics* (New York, 2016), pp. 90–92.

14 Ibid., p. 92.

15 Charles M. Duncan, *Eat, Drink, and Be Wary: How Unsafe Is Our Food?* (Lanham, MD, 2015), pp. 4–5.

16 Jamie Doward and Amy Moore, 'Investigation: Cartels and Organised Crime Target Food in Hunt for Riches', *The Observer* (4 May 2014), pp. 1, 8.

17 Moore, Spink and Lipp, 'Development and Application', pp. R118–R119.

18 Caroline E. Handford, Katrina Campbell and Christopher T. Elliott, 'Impacts of Milk Fraud on Food Safety and Nutrition with Special Emphasis on Developing Countries', *Comprehensive Reviews in Food Science and Food Safety*, XV/1 (January 2016), pp. 136–7.

19 Evershed and Temple, *Sorting the Beef from the Bull*, p. 196.

20 Ibid., pp. 196–7.

21 Fred Gale and Dinghuan Hu, 'Supply Chain Issues in China's Milk Adulteration Incident', paper presented at the International Association of Agricultural Economists' 2009 Conference, Beijing, China, 16–22 August 2009, pp. 1–2.

22 Handford, Campbell and Elliott, 'Impacts of Milk Fraud', pp. 136–7.

23 Karen Everstine, John Spink and Shaun Kennedy, 'Economically Motivated Adulteration (EMA) of Food: Common Characteristics of EMA Incidents', *Journal of Food Protection*, LXXVI/4 (April 2013), pp. 727–8.

24 Patrick J. Lyons, 'Italy's Mozzarella Makers Fight Dioxin Scare', *New York Times*, 21 March 2008, www.nytimes.com.

25 Lawrence M. Schell, Mia V. Gallo and Katsi Cook, 'What's Not to Eat: Food Adulteration in the Context of Human Biology', *American Journal of Human Biology*, xxiv/2 (March 2012), pp. 143–4.

26 Adams, *Food Forensics*, p. 52.

27 Christopher D. Cook, *Diet for a Dead Planet: How the Food Industry Is Killing Us* (New York, 2004), pp. 168–9.

28 Laura Parker, 'Plastic', *National Geographic*, 233 (June 2018), p. 50.

29 Julia Belluz and Radhika Viswanathan, 'The Problem with All the Plastic that's Leaching Into Your Food', www.vox.com, 11 September 2018.

30 Pierre Desrochers and Hiroko Shimizu, *The Locavore's Dilemma: In Praise of the 10,000-mile Diet* (New York, 2012), pp. 154–5.

31 Harris Solomon, 'Unreliable Eating: Patterns of Food Adulteration in Urban India', *BioSocieties*, x/2 (2015), pp. 185–6.

32 Ibid., p. 187.

33 Liza Lin, 'Keeping the Mystery Out of China's Meat', *Companies/ Industries* (24 March–6 April 2014), p. 28.

34 World Health Organization, 'Food Safety: What You Should Know', www.searo.who.int, 7 April 2015.

35 Solomon, 'Unreliable Eating', p. 183.

36 S. M. Solaiman and Abu Noman Mohammad Atahar N. Ali, 'Rampant Food Adulteration in Bangladesh: Gross Violations of Fundamental Human Rights with Impunity', *Asia-Pacific Journal on Human Rights and Law*, xiv/1–2 (2013), p. 33.

37 Sharifa Nasreen and Tahmeed Ahmed, 'Food Adulteration and Consumer Awareness in Dhaka City, 1995–2011', *Journal of Health, Population and Nutrition*, xxxii/3 (September 2014), p. 453.

38 Evershed and Temple, *Sorting the Beef from the Bull*, pp. 258–9.

39 Javaid Bashir, 'Food Adulteration', *Pakistan Observer*, 5 March 2017, www.pakobserver.net.

40 Solaiman and Ali, 'Rampant Food Adulteration in Bangladesh', p. 8.

41 *New Nation* (Dhaka), 20 March 2015.

42 Gautam Anita and Singh Neetu, 'Hazards of New Technology in Promoting Food Adulteration', *Journal of Environmental Science, Toxicology and Food Technology*, v/1 (July–August 2013), pp. 8–9.

43 M. P. Khapre et al., 'Buying Practices and Prevalence of
    Adulteration in Selected Food Items in a Rural Area of Wardha
    District: A Cross-sectional Study', *Online Journal of Health and
    Allied Sciences*, x/3 (July–September 2011), pp. 1–2.

3 COUNTERFEIT FOODS AND COMPLETE SUBSTITUTIONS

 1 Bee Wilson, *Swindled: From Poison Sweets to Counterfeit Coffee –
    The Dark History of the Food Cheats* (London, 2008), pp. 213–15.
 2 Belinda J. Davis, 'Peace Freedom and Bread', in *The World War I
    Reader*, ed. Michael S. Neiberg (New York, 2007), p. 264.
 3 Wilson, *Swindled*, p. 215.
 4 Casey Seidenberg, 'How to Choose a Healthier Mayonnaise,
    or Make Your Own', *Washington Post*, 8 August 2018,
    www.washingtonpost.com.
 5 Jibran Khan, 'The FDA's Attack on Milk Substitutes is Corporate
    Welfare in Action', *National Review*, 1 August 2018,
    www.nationalreview.com.
 6 Richard Evershed and Nicola Temple, *Sorting the Beef from
    the Bull: The Science of Food Fraud Forensics* (New York, 2016),
    p. 188.
 7 Kati Stevens, *Fake* (New York, 2019), p. 24.
 8 Raffi Khatchadourian, 'The Taste Makers', *New Yorker*,
    23 November 2009, www.newyorker.com.
 9 Stevens, *Fake*, p. 42.
10 Stephen Castle and Doreen Carvajal, 'Counterfeit Food More
    Widespread than Suspected', *New York Times*, 26 June 2013,
    www.nytimes.com.
11 Larry Olmsted, *Real Food, Fake Food: Why You Don't Know
    What You're Eating and What You Can Do About It* (Chapel Hill,
    NC, 2016), p. 36.
12 Wenjing Zhang and Jianhong Xue, 'Economically Motivated
    Food Fraud and Adulteration in China: An Analysis Based on
    1,553 Media Reports', *Food Control*, LXVII (2016), p. 196.
13 Roberto A. Ferdman, 'The Wasabi Sushi Restaurants Serve is
    Pretty Much Never Actual Wasabi', *Washington Post*, 15 October
    2014, www.washingtonpost.com.
14 John Spink and Douglas C. Moyer, 'Backgrounder: Defining the
    Public Health Threat of Food Fraud', National Center for Food

Protection and Defense, https://onlinelibrary.wiley.com, 30 April 2011, p. 5.

15 Evershed and Temple, *Sorting the Beef from the Bull*, p. 211.

16 Rich Cohen, 'Inside Quebec's Great, Multi-million-dollar Maple-Syrup Heist', *Vanity Fair*, December 2016, www.vanityfair.com.

17 Patrick Allen, 'Counterfeit Foods, and How to Spot Them', www.lifehacker.com, 10 May 2016.

18 Belle Cushing, 'The 15 Most Common Counterfeit Foods, and How to Identify Them', *Bon Appetit*, 4 February 2014, www.bonappetit.com.

19 Lydia Mulvany, 'The Parmesan Cheese You Sprinkle on Your Penne Could Be Wood', *Bloomberg News*, 16 February 2016, www.bloomberg.com. In the EU, the name Parmesan is protected because of its connection to the Parma region of Italy. See Olmsted, *Real Food, Fake Food*, p. 27.

20 Kimberly Warner et al., 'Deceptive Dishes: Seafood Swaps Found Worldwide', Oceana, http://usa.oceana.org, September 2016, pp. 1, 7.

21 Evershed and Temple, *Sorting the Beef from the Bull*, p. 111.

22 Ibid., pp. 122–3.

23 Oceana, '1 in 5 Seafood Samples Mislabeled Worldwide, Finds New Oceana Report', www.oceana.org, 7 September 2016.

24 Beth Lowell et al., 'One Name, One Fish: Why Seafood Names Matter', www.oceana.org, July 2015.

25 Paul Greenberg, *Four Fish: The Future of the Last Wild Food* (New York, 2010), pp. 82, 84.

26 Lowell et al., 'One Name, One Fish'.

27 Emma Bryce, 'Five Fishy Cases of Seafood Fraud', *Hakai Magazine*, 2 December 2016, www.hakaimagazine.com.

28 Olmsted, *Real Food, Fake Food*, pp. 69–70.

29 Steven Hedlund, 'Seafood FAQ: Langostino vs Lobster: What's the Difference?', www.seafoodsource.com, 1 April 2006.

30 Bryce, 'Five Fishy Cases of Seafood Fraud'.

31 Amie Tsang, 'What, Exactly, Is Meat? Plant-based Food Producers Sue Missouri Over Labeling', *New York Times*, 28 August 2018, www.nytimes.com.

32 Nellie Bowles, 'Got Milk? Or Was That Really a Plant Beverage?', *New York Times*, 31 August 2018, www.nytimes.com.

33 Michael Moss, *Salt, Sugar, Fat: How the Food Giants Hooked Us* (New York, 2013), pp. 162–3.

34 Wise Foods, 'Wise Cheez Doodles', www.cheezdoodles.com, accessed 16 July 2019.

35 Anthony Winson, *The Industrial Diet: The Degradation of Food and the Struggle for Healthy Eating* (New York, 2014), p. 173.

36 Stevens, *Fake*, p. 24.

37 Mark Schatzker, *The Dorito Effect: The Surprising New Truth about Food and Flavor* (New York, 2015), pp. 27–9.

38 Ibid., pp. 63, 230.

4 THE IMPORTANCE OF PLACE

1 Amy B. Trubek, 'The Revolt against Homogeneity', in *Food in Time and Place: The American Historical Association Companion to Food History*, ed. Paul Freedman, Joyce E. Chaplin and Ken Albala (Berkeley, CA, 2014), pp. 307–8.

2 Larry Olmsted, *Real Food, Fake Food: Why You Don't Know What You're Eating and What You Can Do About It* (Chapel Hill, NC, 2016), pp. 169–70.

3 Ibid., pp. 165–6.

4 Ibid., p. 165.

5 Karen Everstine, John Spink and Shaun Kennedy, 'Economically Motivated Adulteration (EMA) of Food: Common Characteristics of EMA Incidents', *Journal of Food Protection*, LXXVI/4 (April 2013), p. 728.

6 Richard Evershed and Nicola Temple, *Sorting the Beef from the Bull: The Science of Food Fraud Forensics* (New York, 2016), p. 231.

7 Tom Mueller, *Extra Virginity: The Sublime and Scandalous World of Olive Oil* (New York, 2012), p. 223.

8 Sonia Soares et al., 'A Comprehensive Review on the Main Honey Authentication Issues: Production and Origin', *Comprehensive Reviews in Food Science and Food Safety*, XVI/5 (September 2017), pp. 1072–3.

9 Rosie Taylor, 'War on Phony Honey: Health Food Giant Will Test All Manuka Jars Before They Go On Sale to Curb the Rising Tide of Cheap Fakes', *Daily Mail*, 31 July 2018, www.dailymail.co.uk.

10 Bernard Lagan, 'Hive of Activity where £100 Manuka Honey is Made', *Sunday Times*, 4 August 2018, www.thetimes.co.uk.

11 Evershed and Temple, *Sorting the Beef from the Bull*, pp. 64–6, 80–81.

12 Olmsted, *Real Food, Fake Food*, pp. 187–92.

13 Quoted ibid., p. 192.

14 Emilie Vandecandelaere, 'Geographic Origin and Identification Labels: Associating Food Quality with Location', in *Innovations in Food Labelling*, ed. Janice Albert, www.fao.org, 2010, p. 145.

15 Denis Stearns, 'A Continuing Plague: Faceless Transactions and the Coincident Rise of Food Adulteration and Legal Regulation of Quality', *Wisconsin Law Review*, CI (2014), p. 425.

16 Natalie O'Neill, 'The Fight for Real Kobe Beef is Coming to a Restaurant Near You', www.eater.com, 9 November 2015.

17 Olmsted, *Real Food, Fake Food*, pp. 132–6.

18 Ibid., pp. 139–40; Mike Pomranz, 'The Vast Majority of Kobe Beef is Fake and Japan Wants to Fix the Problem', *Food and Wine*, 22 June 2017, www.foodandwine.com.

19 O'Neill, 'The Fight for Real Kobe Beef'.

20 'Japan Adds Kobe Beef, Yubari Melons to List of Protected Brands', *Japan Times*, 22 December 2015, www.japantimes.co.jp.

21 Olmsted, *Real Food, Fake Food*, p. 119.

22 World Intellectual Property Organization, 'Geographical Indications: An Introduction', www.wipo.int, 2017, pp. 8, 10.

23 Claudia Dias and Luis Mendes, 'Protected Designation of Origin (PDO), Protected Geographical Indication (PGI) and Traditional Speciality Guaranteed (TSG): A Bibiliometric Analysis', *Food Research International*, 103 (2018), p. 492.

24 European Commission, 'EU Agricultural Product Quality Policy', http://ec.europa.eu, accessed 30 May 2019.

25 Olmsted, *Real Food, Fake Food*, p. 143.

26 Junko Mimura, 'Dawn of Geographical Indications in Japan: Strategic Marketing Management of GI Candidates', paper presented at the 145th EAAE seminar 'Intellectual Property Rights for Geographical Indications: What is at Stake in the TTIP?', 2015, http://ageconsearch.umn.edu; O'Neill, 'The Fight for Real Kobe Beef'.

27 World Intellectual Property Organization, 'Geographical Indications: An Introduction', p. 16.

28 Café de Colombia, 'Colombian Coffee', www.cafedecolombia.com, accessed 30 May 2019.

29 European Commission, 'EU Agricultural Product Quality Policy'.
30 Dias and Mendes, 'Protected Designation of Origin', p. 504.
31 O'Neill, 'The Fight for Real Kobe Beef'.
32 California Champagnes, 'What Is Champagne?',
    www.californiachampagnes.com, accessed 30 May 2019.
33 UNESCO, 'Browse the Lists of Intangible Cultural Heritage
    and the Register of Good Safeguarding Practices',
    http://ich.unesco.org, accessed 30 May 2019.
34 Quoted in Nicola Twilley, 'UNESCO Culinary Heritage Sites',
    www.ediblegeography.com, 9 February 2010.
35 Brian Halweil, *Eat Here: Reclaiming Homegrown Pleasures
    in a Global Supermarket* (New York, 2004), pp. 20–21.
36 Olmsted, *Real Food, Fake Food*, p. 123.
37 Charles Fishman, *The Wal-Mart Effect* (New York, 2006),
    pp. 168–81.
38 Jonathan Rees, *Refrigeration Nation: A History of Ice, Appliances
    and Enterprise in America* (Baltimore, MD, 2013), pp. 192–3.
39 Frederick Kaufman, *Bet the Farm: How Food Stopped Being Food*
    (New York, 2012), p. 16.
40 Pierre Desrochers and Hiroko Shimizu, *The Locavore's Dilemma:
    In Praise of the 10,000-mile Diet* (New York, 2012), pp. 153–7.

5 TESTING

1 Bee Wilson, *Swindled: From Poison Sweets to Counterfeit
   Coffee – The Dark History of the Food Cheats* (London, 2008),
   pp. 116–18.
2 Dadasaheb Navale and Shelley Gupta, 'Analysis of Adulteration
   Present in Milk Products', *International Journal of Latest
   Technology in Engineering, Management and Applied Science*,
   v/6 (June 2016), p. 166.
3 Regi George Jenarius, '41 Ingenious Ways to Quickly Detect
   Adulteration in the Most Common Foods We Eat', *India Times*,
   6 May 2018, www.indiatimes.com.
4 Sofia Griffiths, 'Defining Food Fraud Prevention to Align Food
   Science and Technology Resources', *Journal of the Institute
   of Food Science and Technology*, 12 February 2013,
   http://fstjournal.org.
5 María Pilar Callao and Itziar Ruisánchez, 'An Overview of

Multivariate Qualitative Methods for Food Fraud Detection', *Food Control*, LXXXVI (April 2018), pp. 287, 290.

6 Richard Evershed and Nicola Temple, *Sorting the Beef from the Bull: The Science of Food Fraud Forensics* (New York, 2016), pp. 54–7.

7 Ibid., pp. 59, 64.

8 David I. Ellis et al., 'Point-and-shoot: Rapid Quantitative Detection Methods for On-site Food Fraud Analysis – Moving Out of the Laboratory and Into the Food Supply Chain', *Analytical Methods*, VII/22 (2015), p. 9403.

9 David I. Ellis et al., 'Fingerprinting Food: Current Technologies for the Detection of Food Adulteration and Contamination', *Chemical Society Review*, XLI/17 (2012), pp. 5719–20.

10 Connor Black, 'Innovations in Detecting Food Fraud Using Mass Spectrometric Platforms and Chemometric Modelling', unpublished PhD dissertation, Queen's University Belfast, 2017, p. iii.

11 Ellis et al., 'Fingerprinting Food', pp. 5713–14.

12 Ellis et al., 'Point-and-shoot', p. 9405.

13 Neil Sharma, 'Fighting Food Fraud: Testing Without the Wait', *New Food*, 16 May 2017, www.newfoodmagazine.com.

14 Liza Lin, 'Keeping the Mystery Out of China's Meat', *Companies/Industries* (24 March–6 April 2014), p. 27.

15 Evershed and Temple, *Sorting the Beef from the Bull*, pp. 77, 75, 71–2.

16 Jeffrey Moore, John Spink and Markus Lipp, 'Development and Application of a Database of Food Ingredient Fraud and Economically Motivated Adulteration from 1980 to 2010', *Journal of Food Science*, LXXIV/4 (April 2012), p. R122.

17 Casiane Salete Tibola et al., 'Economically Motivated Food Fraud and Adulteration in Brazil: Incidents and Alternatives to Minimize Occurrence', *Journal of Food Science*, LXXXIII/1 (July 2018), p. 2035.

18 Moore, Spink and Lipp, 'Development and Application', p. R123.

19 Louise Manning and Jan Mei Soon, 'Developing Systems to Control Food Adulteration', *Food Policy*, XLIX/1 (2014), pp. 26, 31.

20 Pamela Galvin-King, Simon A. Haughey and Christopher T. Elliott, 'Herb and Spice Fraud: The Drivers, Challenges and Detection', *Food Control*, LXXXVIII (June 2018), pp. 88–9.

21 Ibid., pp. 91–2.

22 Eunyoung Hong et al., 'Modern Analytical Methods for the Detection of Food Fraud and Adulteration by Food Category', *Journal of the Science of Food and Agriculture*, xcvii/12 (September 2017), pp. 3889–90.

23 Ibid., p. 3882.

24 Georgios P. Danezis et al., 'Food Authentication: Techniques, Trends and Emerging Approaches', *Trends in Analytical Chemistry*, lxxxv (March 2016), p. 124.

25 Evershed and Temple, *Sorting the Beef from the Bull*, p. 136.

26 Ibid., pp. 132–3.

27 Larry Olmsted, *Real Food, Fake Food: Why You Don't Know What You're Eating and What You Can Do About It* (Chapel Hill, nc, 2016), p. 53.

28 Evershed and Temple, *Sorting the Beef from the Bull*, pp. 125–6.

29 Ibid., pp. 166–7.

30 Víctor de Carvalho Martins et al., 'Fraud Investigation in Commercial Coffee by Chromatography', *Food Quality and Safety*, ii/3 (September 2018), pp. 121–3, 129.

31 Victoria Andrea Arana et al., 'Classification of Coffee Beans by gc-c-irms, gc-ms, and 1h-nmr', *Journal of Analytical Methods in Chemistry* (2016), doi 10.1155/2016/8564584.

32 Ibid.

33 Bjørn Pedersen et al., 'Protecting Our Food: Can Standard Food Safety Analysis Detect Adulteration of Food Products with Selected Chemical Agents?', *Trends in Analytical Chemistry*, lxxxv (Part B) (December 2016), pp. 43–4.

34 Evershed and Temple, *Sorting the Beef from the Bull*, pp. 56–7.

6 POLICY, STRATEGY AND LEGISLATION

1 David I. Ellis et al., 'Fingerprinting Food: Current Technologies for the Detection of Food Adulteration and Contamination', *Chemical Society Review*, xli/17 (2012), p. 5706.

2 Sharifa Nasreen and Tahmeed Ahmed, 'Food Adulteration and Consumer Awareness in Dhaka City, 1995–2011', *Journal of Health, Population and Nutrition*, xxxii/3 (September 2014), pp. 453, 463.

3 Gazi Delwar Hosen and Syed Robayet Ferdous, 'The Role of Mobile Courts in the Enforcement of Laws in Bangladesh', *Northern University Journal of Law*, 1 (2010), pp. 82, 87.

4 Nasreen and Ahmed, 'Food Adulteration', p. 459.

5 Ibid., p. 456.

6 Julfikar Ali Manik and Ashutosh Sarkar, 'Govt Sits On Setting Up Food Courts', *Daily Star* (Bangladesh), 1 July 2013, www.thedailystar.net.

7 Government Accountability Office, 'Experiences of Seven Countries in Consolidating Their Food Safety Systems', GAO-05-212, www.gao.gov, 22 February 2005, p. 1.

8 National Food Crime Unit, www.food.gov.uk.

9 Anthony Winson, *The Industrial Diet: The Degradation of Food and the Struggle for Healthy Eating* (New York, 2014), p. 173.

10 John Spink and Douglas C. Moyer, 'Defining the Public Health Threat of Food Fraud', *Journal of Food Science*, LXXIX/9 (November–December 2011), p. R160.

11 Richard Evershed and Nicola Temple, *Sorting the Beef from the Bull: The Science of Food Fraud Forensics* (New York, 2016), pp. 22–3.

12 Sandra Hoffmann and William Harder, 'Food Safety and Risk Governance in Globalized Markets', *Health Matrix*, XX/1 (2012), p. 8.

13 World Health Organization: Bangladesh, 'Food Safety', www.searo.who.int, accessed 31 May 2019.

14 Hoffmann and Harder, 'Food Safety and Risk Governance', pp. 24–7.

15 United Nations Food and Agriculture Organization, 'What is the Codex Alimentarius?', www.fao.org.

16 Karen Everstine et al., 'Development of a Hazard Classification Scheme for Substances Used in Fraudulent Adulteration of Foods', *Journal of Food Protection*, LXXXI/1 (January 2018), p. 32.

17 United States Pharmacopeial Convention, 'Decernis Acquires Food Fraud Database from USP', 15 June 2018, www.usp.org.

18 Louise Manning, 'Food Fraud: Policy and Food Chain', *Current Opinion in Food Science*, X (2016), p. 18.

19 Qi Tang et al., 'Food Traceability Systems in China: The Current Status of and Future Perspectives on Food Supply Chain Databases, Legal Support, and Technological Research and

Support for Food Safety Regulation', *BioScience Trends*, IX/1 (February 2015), p. 7.

20 European Commission, 'Food Law General Requirements', http://ec.europa.eu, accessed 31 May 2019.

21 FISH-BOL, 'Vision for FISH-BOL', www.fishbol.org, accessed 31 May 2019.

22 Eunyoung Hong et al., 'Modern Analytical Methods for the Detection of Food Fraud and Adulteration by Food Category', *Journal of the Science of Food and Agriculture*, XCVII/12 (September 2017), p. 3883.

23 Produce Marketing Association, 'Traceability and FSMA', www.pma.com, May 2014.

24 'Counterfeit Food', *Chemistry and Industry* (January 2015), p. 21.

25 Global Food Safety Initiative, 'What Is GSFI', www.mygfsi.com, accessed 31 May 2019.

26 John Spink et al., 'Food Fraud Prevention: Policy, Strategy, and Decision-making – Implementation Steps for a Government Agency or Industry', *Chimia*, LXX/5 (May 2016), p. 324.

27 Liza Lin, 'Keeping the Mystery Out of China's Meat', *Companies/Industries* (24 March–6 April 2014), p. 27.

28 Ibid., pp. 27–8.

29 Evershed and Temple, *Sorting the Beef from the Bull*, p. 286.

30 Steve Lapidge, 'Fighting Food Fraud to Protect Brand Australia', *Australian Science* (March–April 2018), p. 39, www.australasianscience.com.au.

31 True Source Honey, www.truesourcehoney.com.

32 Evershed and Temple, *Sorting the Beef from the Bull*, p. 37.

33 Josh Long, 'Groups Criticize Trump's Plan to Reduce FDA Food-Safety Budget', *Food Insider Journal*, www.foodinsiderjournal.com, 25 May 2017.

34 John Spink et al., 'Food Fraud Prevention Shifts the Food Risk Focus to Vulnerability', *Trends in Food Science and Technology*, LXII (April 2017), pp. 216–17, 219.

35 Denis W. Stearns, 'A Continuing Plague: Faceless Transactions and the Coincident Rise of Food Adulteration and Legal Regulation of Quality', *Wisconsin Law Review*, 421 (2014), pp. 440–42.

36 International Food Information Council (IFIC) and U.S. Food
    and Drug Administration (FDA), 'Overview of Food Ingredients,
    Additives and Colors', www.fda.gov, April 2010.
37 Charles M. Duncan, *Eat, Drink, and Be Wary: How Unsafe Is
    Our Food?* (Lanham, MD, 2015), p. 93.
38 European Commission, 'Questions and Answers on Food
    Additives', http://europa.eu, 14 November 2011.
39 Melissa Kravitz, '6 Foods that are Legal in the U.S. but Banned
    in Other Countries', *Business Insider*, 1 March 2017,
    www.businessinsider.com.
40 Everstine et al., 'Development of a Hazard Classification Scheme',
    pp. 31–2.
41 European Commission, 'General Food Law', https://ec.europa.
    eu/food/safety/general_food_law_en, accessed 30 May 2019.
42 Regulations as quoted in Everstine et al., 'Development of a
    Hazard Classification Scheme', pp. 31–2.
43 Duncan, *Eat, Drink, and Be Wary*, p. 57.

CONCLUSION: ADULTERATION AND CULTURE

1 Dwight Eschliman and Steve Ettinger, *Ingredients: A Visual
   Exploration of 75 Additives and 25 Food Products* (New York,
   2015), p. 154.
2 Center for Science in the Public Interest, 'Sodium Benzoate,
   Benzoic Acid', Chemical Cuisine, https://cspinet.org, accessed
   17 May 2019.
3 EFSA ANS Panel (EFSA Panel on Food Additives and Nutrient
   Sources Added to Food), 'Scientific Opinion on the
   Re-evaluation of Benzoic Acid (E 210), Sodium Benzoate (E 211),
   Potassium Benzoate (E 212) and Calcium Benzoate (E 213) as
   Food Additives', *EFSA Journal* (2016), p. 110, www.efsa.europa.eu.
4 'Panera Removes Artificial Ingredients from U.S. Menu',
   www.reuters.com, 13 January 2017.
5 Quoted in Daniela Galarza, 'Twitter Drags Panera for Ill-
   informed Tweet about Food Additives', www.eater.com, 24 July
   2017.
6 Ibid.
7 Derek Lowe, 'Sodium Benzoate Nonsense', In the Pipeline blog,
   Science Magazine, 24 June 2017, http://blogs.sciencemag.org.

8   Ibid.

9   James E. McWilliams, *Just Food: Where Locavores Get It Wrong and How We Can Truly Eat Responsibly* (New York, 2009), p. 66.

10 Marion Nestle, *Safe Food: The Politics of Food Safety*, 2nd edn (Berkeley, CA, 2010), pp. 207–13.

11 John T. Lang, *What's So Controversial about Genetically Modified Food?* (London, 2016), p. 73.

12 Andrew F. Smith, *Eating History: Thirty Turning Points in the Making of American Cuisine* (New York, 2009), p. 282.

13 Nestle, *Safe Food*, p. 225. A 2016 law in the United States in fact mandated the labelling of genetically modified foods, but the Trump administration has effectively blocked its enforcement. See Chelsey Davis, 'GMO Labeling May be Dead on Arrival Due to Trump Requirement', www.tracegains.com, 15 March 2017.

14 David H. Freedman, 'The Truth about Genetically Modified Food', *Scientific American*, 1 September 2012, www.scientificamerican.com; 'Plant Biotechnology: Tarnished Promise', *Nature*, CDXCVII/21 (2 May 2013), www.nature.com.

15 Kati Stevens, *Fake* (New York, 2019), p. 39.

16 Freedman, 'The Truth about Genetically Modified Food'.

17 Lorraine Chow, 'Gene-edited Products Now Classified as GMOs in European Union', www.ecowatch.com, 25 July 2018.

18 Yi Li, 'These CRISPR-modified Crops Don't Count as GMOs', 22 May 2018, theconversation.com.

19 Paul Enriquez, 'CRISPR GMOs', *North Carolina Journal of Law and Technology*, XXVIII/4 (May 2017), p. 473. See also Freedman, 'The Truth about Genetically Modified Food'.

20 Jan M. Lucht, 'Public Acceptance of Plant Biotechnology and GM Crops', *Viruses*, VII/8 (August 2015), pp. 4268–9.

21 Jake Johnson, 'Study Reveals "Large-scale Illegal Presence" of GMOs in India's Food Supply', www.ecowatch.com, 31 July 2018.

22 Robby Berman, 'Is the American Public Finally Okay with GMOs? Um . . .', www.bigthink.com, 18 August 2018.

23 Lucht, 'Public Acceptance', pp. 4256, 4259.

24 Malcolm Gladwell, 'The Imaginary Crimes of Margit Hamosh', *Revisionist History* (podcast), season three, episode 8, www.revisionisthistory.com.

25 Ibid.; Malcolm Gladwell, 'Department of Straight Thinking: Is

the Belgian Coca-Cola Hysteria the Real Thing?', *New Yorker*, 12 July 1999, http://archives.newyorker.com.

26 H. Kendall et al., 'Food Fraud and the Perceived Integrity of European Food Imports into China', *PLOS ONE*, XIII/5 (2018), pp. 3, 10, 20.

27 Paul Greenberg, *Four Fish: The Future of the Last Wild Food* (New York, 2010), p. 250.

28 Sarah Lohman, *Eight Flavors: The Untold Story of American Cuisine* (New York, 2016), pp. 197–8.

29 Jeffrey Kluger, 'Inside the Food Labs,' *Time*, 28 December 2003, www.time.com.

30 Andrew F. Smith, *Fast Food: The Good, the Bad and the Hungry* (London, 2016), pp. 38, 40.

31 Annie Gasparro and Heather Haddon, 'Anyone for Diglycerides? Anyone? Food Scientists are Getting Fed Up with Picky Eaters', *Wall Street Journal*, 12 October 2018, www.wsj.com.

32 Bee Wilson, *Swindled: From Poison Sweets to Counterfeit Coffee – The Dark History of the Food Cheats* (London, 2008), pp. 322–3.

33 Stevens, *Fake*, p. 34.

34 Rachel Laudan, 'A Plea for Culinary Modernism: Why We Should Love New, Fast, Processed Food', *Gastronomica*, I/1 (February 2001), p. 40.

35 Lana Bandoim, 'Why McDonald's Got Rid of Artificial Additives in its Burgers', *Fortune*, 27 September 2018, www.forbes.com.

36 Ibid.

NOTE ON SOURCES AND SELECT BIBLIOGRAPHY

I am a historian by training and by inclination. I started this book while finishing a biography of Harvey Washington Wiley, the first head of what would eventually be known as the United States Food and Drug Administration. At the turn of the twentieth century, Wiley had to wrestle with all sorts of philosophical questions regarding the nature of adulteration in foods of all kinds. I quickly realized that many of those questions remain just as pertinent today as they did during Wiley's lifetime. Since there was not enough space in that book for me to cover the debate over those questions both then and now, I decided to write this book too. Many thanks to Andy Smith, Michael Leaman and everyone at Reaktion Books for offering me a way to explore those issues more deeply here. Research for each of these books greatly improved the other.

Before listing my most important sources, I wanted to highlight two books for their particular influence on my thinking in this subject. Larry Olmsted's *Real Food, Fake Food: Why You Don't Know What You're Eating and What You Can Do About It* (Chapel Hill, NC, 2016) appears in the footnotes for many chapters of this book, but is the fundamental bedrock of Chapter Five. *Sorting the Beef from the Bull: The Science of Food Fraud Forensics* by Richard Evershed and Nicola Temple (New York, 2016) is for obvious reasons a crucial source for Chapter Six, on testing, but it is also an excellent starting place for anybody who wants to learn more about the science of food adulteration than I could possibly tell them.

I was surprised by the huge number of scientific papers written on food adulteration in even just the last five years. I cannot pretend to have read all of them, but I have read enough to feel I understand the relationship between science, nature and culture that impacts exactly how people around the world perceive this problem. The books and articles I list below are the ones that I found most helpful; if a source was used only once in the book, it will appear in the References and not here.

BOOKS

Adams, Mike, *Food Forensics: The Hidden Toxins Lurking in Your Food and How You Can Avoid them for Lifelong Health* (Dallas, TX, 2016)

Desrochers, Pierre, and Hiroko Shimizu, *The Locavore's Dilemma: In Praise of the 10,000-mile Diet* (New York, 2012)

Duncan, Charles M., *Eat, Drink, and Be Wary: How Unsafe is Our Food?* (Lanham, MD, 2015)

Greenberg, Paul, *Four Fish: The Future of the Last Wild Food* (New York, 2010)

Lohman, Sarah, *Eight Flavors: The Untold Story of American Cuisine* (New York, 2016)

Mueller, Tom, *Extra Virginity: The Sublime and Scandalous World of Olive Oil* (New York, 2012)

Nestle, Marion, *Safe Food: The Politics of Food Safety*, 2nd edn (Berkeley, CA, 2010)

Schatzker, Mark, *The Dorito Effect: The Surprising New Truth about Food and Flavor* (New York, 2015)

Stevens, Kati, *Fake* (New York, 2019)

Wilson, Bee, *Swindled: From Poison Sweets to Counterfeit Coffee – The Dark History of the Food Cheats* (London, 2008)

Winson, Anthony, *The Industrial Diet: The Degradation of Food and the Struggle for Healthy Living* (New York, 2014)

ARTICLES AND REPORTS

Arana, Victoria Andrea, et al., 'Classification of Coffee Beans by GC-C-IRMS, GC-MS, and 1H-NMR', *Journal of Analytical Methods in Chemistry* (2016), DOI: 10.1155/2016/8564584

Bandoim, Lana, 'Why McDonald's Got Rid of Artificial Additives in its Burgers', *Fortune*, 27 September 2018, www.forbes.com

Castle, Stephen, and Doreen Carvajal, 'Counterfeit Food More

Widespread than Suspected', *New York Times*, 26 June 2013, www.nytimes.com

Davidson, Rebecca K., et al., 'From Food Defence to Food Supply Chain Integrity', *British Food Journal*, CXIX/1 (2017), pp. 52–66

Dias, Claudia, and Luis Mendes, 'Protected Designation of Origin (PDO), Protected Geographical Indication (PGI) and Tradition al Speciality Guaranteed (TSG): A Bibiliometric Analysis', *Food Research International*, CIII (January 2018), pp. 492–508

Ellis, David I., et al., 'Fingerprinting Food: Current Technologies for the Detection of Food Adulteration and Contamination', *Chemical Society Review*, XLI/17 (2012), pp. 5569–868

—, et al., 'Point-and-shoot: Rapid Quantitative Detection Methods for On-site Food Fraud Analysis – Moving Out of the Laboratory and Into the Food Supply Chain', *Analytical Methods*, VII/22 (2015), pp. 9401–14

Everstine, Karen, John Spink and Shaun Kennedy, 'Economically Motivated Adulteration (EMA) of Food: Common Characteristics of EMA Incidents', *Journal of Food Protection*, LXXVI/4 (April 2013), pp. 723–35

—, et al., 'Development of a Hazard Classification Scheme for Substances Used in the Fraudulent Adulteration of Foods', *Journal of Food Protection*, LXXXI/1 (January 2018), pp. 31–6

Galvin-King, Pamela, Simon A. Haughey and Christopher T. Elliott, 'Herb and Spice Fraud: The Drivers, Challenges and Detection', *Food Control*, LXXXVIII (June 2018), pp. 85–97

Handford, Caroline E., Katrina Campbell and Christopher T. Elliott, 'Impacts of Milk Fraud on Food Safety and Nutrition with Special Emphasis on Developing Countries', *Comprehensive Reviews in Food Science and Food Safety*, XV/1 (January 2016), pp. 130–42

Hoffmann, Sandra, and Harder, William, 'Food Safety and Risk Governance in Globalized Markets', *Health Matrix*, XX/1 (2012), pp. 5–53

Hong, Eunyoung, et al., 'Modern Analytical Methods for the Detection of Food Fraud and Adulteration by Food Category', *Journal of the Science of Food and Agriculture*, XCVII/12 (2017), pp. 3877–96

Johnson, Renée, 'Food Fraud and "Economically Motivated
    Adulteration" of Food and Food Ingredients', *Congressional
    Research Service*, 10 January 2014

Lin, Liza, 'Keeping the Mystery Out of China's Meat', *Companies/
    Industries* (24 March–6 April 2014), pp. 27–9

Lotta, Francesca, and Joe Bogue, 'Defining Food Fraud in the
    Modern Supply Chain', *European Food and Feed Law Review*,
    x/2 (2015), pp. 114–22

Lucht, Jan M., 'Public Acceptance of Plant Biotechnology and
    GM Crops', *Viruses*, VII/8 (August 2015), pp. 4254–81

Manning, Louise, and Jan Mei Soon, 'Food Safety, Food Fraud,
    and Food Defense: A Fast Evolving Literature', *Journal of
    Food Science*, LXXXI/4 (April 2016), pp. R823–R834

Matthews, Susan, 'You Don't Need to Worry about Roundup in
    Your Breakfast Cereal', www.slate.com, 16 August 2018

Moore, Jeffrey C., John Spink and Markus Lipp, 'Development
    and Application of a Database of Food Ingredient Fraud and
    Economically Motivated Adulteration from 1980 to 2010', *Journal
    of Food Science*, LXXVII/4 (April 2012), pp. R118–R126

Nasreen, Sharifa, and Tahmeed Ahmed, 'Food Adulteration and
    Consumer Awareness in Dhaka City, 1995–2011', *Journal of
    Health, Population and Nutrition*, 32/3 (September 2014),
    pp. 452–64

O'Neill, Natalie, 'The Fight for Real Kobe Beef is Coming to a
    Restaurant Near You', www.eater.com, 9 November 2015

Soares, Sonia, et al.. 'A Comprehensive Review on the Main Honey
    Authentication Issues: Production and Origin', *Comprehensive
    Reviews in Food Science and Food Safety*, XVI/5 (September 2017),
    pp. 1072–100

Solaiman, S. M., and Abu Noman Mohammad Atahar N. Ali,
    'Extensive Food Adulteration in Bangladesh: A Violation
    of Fundamental Human Rights and the State's Binding
    Obligations', University of Wollongong Research Online,
    https://ro.uow.edu.au, 2014

Solomon, Harris, 'Unreliable Eating: Patterns of Food Adulteration
    in Urban India', *BioSocieties*, x (2015), pp. 177–93

Spink, John, and Douglas C. Moyer, 'Defining the Public Health
    Threat of Food Fraud', *Journal of Food Science*, LXXVI/9
    (November–December 2011), pp. R157–R163

Stearns, Denis W., 'A Continuing Plague: Faceless Transactions and the Coincident Rise of Food Adulteration and Legal Regulation of Quality', *Wisconsin Law Review*, CI (2014), pp. 421–43

World Intellectual Property Organization, 'Geographical Indications: An Introduction', 2017

PODCASTS

Gladwell, Malcolm, 'The Imaginary Crimes of Margit Hamosh', *Revisionist History*, season three, episode 8, www.revisionisthistory.com

Graber, Cynthia, and Nicola Twilley, 'Fake Food', *Gastropod*, season eight, 6 June 2017, www.gastropod.com

INDEX

Agreement on Trade-related
    Aspects of Intellectual
    Property Rights (TRIPS) 86
Ahmed, Tahmeed 109–11
almond milk 72–3
apple juice 10
Argentina 131
artificial cheese 63, 65
artificial colourants 11
Australia 82, 119–20

Bangladesh 9, 57, 109–11, 114
Belgium 136
benzoic acid *see* sodium
    benzoate
bisphenol A (BPA) 53
Brazil 100, 131
bread 7, 25
buffalo mozzarella 52

cake mix 21
Canada 67–8, 111, 131
caviar 10
Center for Science in the Public
    Interest 126
champagne 77–9, 84, 89
Champagne (French region)
    77–9, 89

cheese puffs 65, 73–4
chemometrics 100
chicory 61
Chile 90–91
chilli powder 9, 50
China 30, 36, 42–3, 66, 118–19,
    132, 137
    melamine scandal in 49–50,
        55, 102
'Chinese Restaurant Syndrome'
    42
chocolate 80
Clustered Regularly Interspaced
    Short Palindromic Repeats
    (CRISPR) 133
Coca-Cola 34, 136
Codex Alimentarius Commission
    (CAC) 114
coffee 105
Colombian coffee 87–8,
    105–6
contamination 16
crab 71
Czech Republic 65, 135

Delaney Clause 122
Denmark 111

Enriquez, Paul 134
Environmental Working Group 43–4
ersatz foods 60–62
European Food Safety Authority (EFSA) 43
European Union (EU) 28, 35–6, 51, 88–9, 123–4, 126, 129
Evershed, Richard 39, 98, 105, 107, 119, 164

farmers 7
First World War 60–61
fish 26, 52–3, 68–72, 90–91, 96, 104–5, 116
Fish Barcode of Life Initiative (FISH-BOL) 116–17
Flavr Savr tomato 130
flour 7
food additives 12, 23, 24, 45
food adulteration, definition of 10
    see also substitutions, poisons, food additives
Food and Drug Administration (FDA) 10, 72, 120, 122, 130, 164
food documentation 18
food fraud, definition of 13–14
    see also substitutions, point of origin fraud
Food Safety Modernization Act 117
foodborne illness 54
France 77–9, 81, 135

General Food Law 124
generic drugs 66

genetically modified organisms (GMOS) 130–35
Geographic Indicator (GI) 86–7
Germany 60–61, 111, 135
Givaudan 64
Global Food Safety Initiative (GFSI) 118
Government Accountability Office (GAO) 111
Great Britain 9, 25, 47, 120
Greece 81, 88
Grocery Manufacturers Association 9, 131
Gruyère 83–4
Gruyères (Swiss town) 83–4

Hassall, Arthur Hill 109
honey 9, 15, 31–2, 68, 82, 96, 98
horse meat 29
hot dogs 39
Hungary 135

ice 26
India 50, 54–6, 58, 132, 134, 139
Ireland 111
Italy 52, 81–2

Japan 63, 86–7, 91, 139
juice 34–5
Just Mayo 62, 73

Kobe beef 85–7
Kobe Beef Association 86
Korbel 77–8
Kraft Macaroni & Cheese 122–3
Kwok, Robert Ho Man 42

labelling 34–6
Lapidge, Stephen 120

Lappé, Frances Moore 37
Laudan, Rachel 141
lecithin 38
Li, Yi 133
Lipp, Markus 16
Lowe, Derek 127
Lyons, Rob 129

McDonald's 139, 142–3
Manouri cheese 88
maple syrup 67–8
Markham, Peter 25
mass spectrometry 99
Matthews, Susan 43–4
meat 29–30, 39–40
melamine 49–50, 55, 102
melons 92
milk 9, 26, 27, 94–5
mislabelling 17
Mitchell, John 94–5
mobile food courts 110–11
monosodium glutamate (MSG) 42

Nasreen, Sharifa 109–11
National Food Crime Unit 112
Netherlands 112
New Zealand 82–3, 112
Norway 89–90

olive oil 9, 17, 20, 28, 68, 81–2
Olmsted, Larry 83, 90, 164
orange juice 39
Oreo cookies 63, 65, 73

Pakistan 25, 57
Panera Bread 126–7, 143
parmesan cheese 68

pesticide residue 19
pizza 63, 75, 89, 92
Pizza Hut 139
point of origin fraud 80–84
poisons 46–54
preservatives 18
Protected Designation of Origin 88

raman spectroscopy 99
Red Lobster 71
Ricardo, David 91
rice 10
risk management 100

saffron 29, 103
Schatzker, Mark 75
Singapore 139
sodium benzoate 126–8
Solomon, Harris 54, 56
soy milk 72
Spain 47, 81, 135
spices 28–9, 67
Starbucks 22, 139
Stearns, Dennis 21
Stephens, Kati 63–4
substitutions 28–31, 101–4
sugar 32
Switzerland 135

Temple, Nicola 39, 98, 105, 107, 119, 164
terroir 79
Thailand 139
thresholds 44
Toxic Oil Syndrome 47
traceability 115–16
Traditional Specialities Guaranteed 87

trans-shipments 17, 81
Tunisia 81
turmeric 58, 103

United Kingdom 112, 135
   see also Great Britain
United Nations Educational,
   Scientific and Cultural
   Organization (UNESCO) 89
United Nations Food and
   Agriculture Organization
   (FAO) 84, 114, 130
United States 18, 22, 71–2, 131
   cultural priorities in 35,
      122–3, 129, 140
   food inspection in 104
   food safety in 117, 120
   wines in 77–8

United States Pharmacopeial
   Convention (USP) 114

vodka 65

Walmart 116
wasabi 67
Washington Post 62
water 16, 26, 27
whisky 11, 37
Wilson, Bee 140
wine 82, 88
Winson, Anthony 23, 74, 112
Wise Foods 73–4
Worcester sauce 51
World Health Organization
   (WHO) 113, 130
World Wildlife Federation 72